Pagan Portals
What Is
Modern Witchcraft?

Pagan Portals
What Is
Modern Witchcraft?

Edited by Trevor Greenfield

MOON
BOOKS

Winchester, UK
Washington, USA

First published by Moon Books, 2019
Moon Books is an imprint of John Hunt Publishing Ltd., No. 3 East Street, Alresford
Hampshire SO24 9EE, UK
office1@jhpbooks.net
www.johnhuntpublishing.com
www.moon-books.net

For distributor details and how to order please visit the 'Ordering' section on our website.

Text copyright: Trevor Greenfield 2018

ISBN: 978 1 78535 866 1
978 1 78535 867 8 (ebook)
Library of Congress Control Number: 2018940515

A CIP catalogue record for this book is available from the British Library.

Design: Stuart Davies

Printed and bound by CPI Group (UK) Ltd, Croydon, CR0 4YY, UK
US: Printed and bound by Edwards Brothers Malloy 15200 NBN Way #B, Blue Ridge Summit,
PA 17214, USA

Other Books in the Series
What is Shamanism?
978-1-78535-802-9 (paperback) 978-1-78535-803-6 (e-book)

We operate a distinctive and ethical publishing philosophy in
all areas of our business, from our global network of authors to
production and worldwide distribution.

Contents

What is Modern Witchcraft?

Morgan Daimler

One of the most intriguing movements gaining popularity today is witchcraft, yet it is also one of the most diverse and difficult to clearly define. For some people witchcraft is a practice, a set of actions designed to create results, while for many others particularly within neopaganism, witchcraft is a religion. Those who feel drawn to this practice or spirituality may think that it will be easy to learn about, and indeed there are a plethora of resources on the market for a seeker to learn from; however, it quickly becomes apparent that what seems like a simple thing to learn about is much more complicated. Modern witchcraft can be nebulous and hard to pin down, but it is also a deeply rewarding thing for those who find a home in it. The key, perhaps, is to be willing to learn about different kinds of witchcraft with an open mind.

Modern witchcraft can be viewed as one path, and it is often discussed as such and forms one generally cohesive wider community. But in the details, a person will find that it can vary greatly from one tradition to another, from one person to another, so that across the broad spectrum of modern witchcraft there is a full array of different beliefs and practices within that wider community. I might suggest that in many ways it is like a tree, where there are many branches, some growing close together, some very far apart, yet all are part of the same living, growing organism. Everyone who identifies as a witch belongs to this wider community, this tree, but our particular branches may be very far apart in many practical respects.

When one is first seeking to understand what witchcraft is it can be difficult to know where to start, simply because of this diversity. However, despite the range of specifics there are some

1

general things we can say about modern witchcraft as it is most often expressed across these different traditions. It is best to remember that there will always be exceptions and that nothing here is meant to be definitive for all kinds of witchcraft. One of the most beautiful things about witchcraft today is its flexibility and diversity because this allows people to find the exact set of beliefs and practices that work for them. Some might see this flexibility as a weakness, but the history of witchcraft seems to prove it is a strength. Certainly it speaks to the viability of witchcraft, that it survived persecution and repression to grow from a small, obscure practice in the mid-twentieth century into the widespread and varied forms we see today.

Perhaps the first and hardest question to answer when we are looking at what modern witchcraft is, is what is a witch? And here we immediately come to an example of the diversity of the community, because there is no single answer. For some people a witch is someone who practices magic. For others a witch is someone who has been initiated into a specific witchcraft tradition or practice, while some may argue that a witch belongs to a specific tradition but doesn't require initiation. For yet others a witch is any person who declares themselves a witch, whether or not they believe or practice anything specific. This may seem confusing but it demonstrates the freedom that is inherent in modern witchcraft, where a person is not limited by other people's definitions unless they choose to be.

A religious or spiritual aspect to witchcraft is one thread that we often see shared among different modern witchcraft approaches. While there are some who take an atheistic or agnostic approach, the majority of modern witchcraft traditions, and modern witches, tend to approach their witchcraft from a deistic perspective. This can include monotheism but most often is polytheism, often predicated on the worship of a specific set of deities. Probably the most common approach in modern neopagan witchcraft is to pair a God and Goddess, sometimes with the Goddess in a primary role, and have this pair as the main focus of worship. In theistic witchcraft the deity or deities being honored are the core of the belief system and are also often vital to the magic being practiced, being called on or invoked in spell work to empower the magic. There is no right or wrong to how divinity can be included in witchcraft, if it is, even, and although the God and Goddess combination is the most common we also see people who focus exclusively on a single God or Goddess, without denying the existence of other deities, or who include three or more deities in their worship. Some people don't have any set deities they honor but rather may focus on a pantheon but change who they are calling on at different times, and others choose a deity based on a specific need. There are probably as many ways to look at including spirituality in witchcraft as there are kinds of witchcraft.

Another common theme of modern witchcraft is the celebration of holidays, particularly among those previously mentioned who take a strongly theistic approach. Which holidays are celebrated will vary from one practice to another, however, in modern neopagan witchcraft the Wheel of the Year is the template most people use. This system gives us a holiday roughly every six weeks, four based on astrological events and four based on the older Irish fire festivals. The names of the holidays on this Wheel will vary by group so what follows is only the most commonly used names; in no way is this meant to imply that these are more genuine. By most reckonings the old year ends and the New Year begins at Samhain, on or around 31 October. This is followed at the winter solstice by Yule, which acknowledges the longest night and shortest day of the year. After that we move to Imbolc, on 1 February, a celebration of the first stirring of spring, followed by Ostara at the spring equinox. These holidays comprise what is often considered the dark half of the year, or winter, beyond this point the Wheel turns to the light half of the year, or summer. The light half begins at Beltane on 1 May which is a celebration of the renewal of life and usually has themes of fertility. On the summer solstice there is Litha or Midsummer, an acknowledgement of the longest day and shortest night. This is followed by Lughnasa on 1 August which is a celebration of the harvest, then, on the autumn equinox there is Mabon, the second harvest and a time to honor the balance between darkness and light. From this point we have circled the entire Wheel and come back again to Samhain, starting the cycle all over again.

In addition to these solar holidays most neopagan witches also celebrate the phases of the moon, particularly the full moon each month. For many neopagan witch traditions the moon is seen as both a symbol of the Goddess and of the witch's power, symbolically, and the belief is that the full moon is the best time for all acts of magic. It is also seen as an ideal time for a variety of related activities like charging crystals and tools, divination, and personal empowerment. Additionally some will also acknowledge the dark moon, although that is not as common.

Tools are another thing that can be found across the breadth of different witchcraft traditions although as with everything else they can vary widely. The concept behind a tool in witchcraft is that it is a physical object that contains or can be used to direct a witch's energy, usually for magical working. For some traditions the main tool will be the athame, or ritual knife; although it is usually a double-sided blade in most traditions it is not used to physically cut anything. Rather this tool is symbolic of the witch's personal power and is used to direct energy during workings as well as to store energy. In many cases the ritual knife is black handled, and some groups require that the knife be made by the witch. Although in older traditions the athame was supposed to be made from iron. In newer forms of witchcraft athames can be stone, wood, or even ceramic, if that is what the witch prefers. Some witches favor using a wand more than a ritual blade, and wands can be made from many different kinds of wood, in whatever form the witch prefers. In modern witchcraft people also choose to make wands from alternative materials including crystal and metal. Another popular tool is the cauldron, which can be used for a variety of purposes, including ritual and spell work, and is often used to represent the Goddess. Beyond these three common tools there are a variety of other tools a witch might choose to use or a tradition might require; some stay simple and minimal while others prefer quantity and variety. Ultimately there is no right or wrong with a witch's tools and modern witches seem eager to both stay traditional and also to explore new and innovative options in working magic and practicing their religion. Tools are often kept on a witch's altar but some people may choose to store them safely away and only bring them out as needed.

Witchcraft has always been a practice that can be isolating to those who follow it, and historically we see many witches who were individual practitioners, but while there are still solitary witches today, modern witches seem more drawn to community and interaction with others. Social media and technology are a different sort of tool of the modern witch, allowing people who are physically or demographically isolated in their daily lives to connect with likeminded people around the world, even. In this aspect more than any other modern witchcraft is truly evolving from its historic roots and the Internet has been probably the greatest impetus in the huge growth recently in the religion. People have an unprecedented access to information on witchcraft and the ability for anyone to share their own practices and beliefs has allowed for the proliferation of modern traditions and practices. People who are isolated from other witches can still participate in the wider community and those who feel that one community doesn't quite suit them can look for another. This may not eradicate the loneliness caused by a lack of physical, in-person associations but it does help ease it. Online discussion forums and social media groups allow for people to reach out and talk to each other, to ask questions, to share information, and to discuss topics relating to witchcraft with people from many different backgrounds and traditions. There are options now for people to take classes online, to live chat with mentors, and I have even seen people coordinate magical workings and religious rituals across the globe using social media. YouTube has channels created by people seeking to share information or offering teaching videos. Technology has been a huge step forward in connecting modern witches to each other and in giving us a larger sense of community beyond the bounds of our own home or neighborhood.

Magic is possibly the strongest link between different forms of modern witchcraft, although as with everything else it isn't ubiquitous. Magic in witchcraft can run the gamut from that based heavily on ceremonial magic to that which is rooted in folk magic, but the core concept is always the same. Magic in witchcraft is done with the intent to bring about change in some form or another, as Aleister Crowley explained it magic is "the Science and Art of causing Change to occur in conformity with Will." For witchcraft, magic can take many forms from structured spells to simple visualizations, all based in this idea of creating change aligned with the witch's will or intention. How complex or how straightforward the practice of magic itself will be will depend on the witch or tradition, but magic itself, both believing in it as a power and using it in one's life tend to be common basic concepts across different kinds of modern witchcraft.

Witches work magic using herbs and oils, tools and candles, but the modern witch might also utilize meditation techniques and eastern healing modalities. The practice of magic, like witchcraft itself, has an endless number of expressions and styles all of which can be found in modern witchcraft. Some will be based heavily or entirely in a specific culture and its folk magic; others may be entirely intuitive and based on the individual witch's instincts and perceptions. Ultimately witchcraft is a pragmatic path, whatever form it takes, and tends to focus on doing what works, and repeating what has proven results.

Modern technology has also blended with magic to move the modern witch into the entirely new and innovative realm of techno-magic. A quick online search will show digital tarot decks, apps for oracles, and a plethora of witchcraft e-books. There are even virtual covens and temples that people can join and participate in. As many of us become more and more focused on technology in our daily lives we are finding ways to express our spirituality in that format and to practice our magic there as well.

This is a general overview of modern witchcraft as it is most often practiced. It should be kept in mind of course that these are only generalities and a seeker will need to take time to explore specific traditions and paths to find the one that suits them best. There is no rigid orthodoxy or even orthopraxy within witchcraft. For every ten witches who worship deities there will be at least one who doesn't acknowledge them. For all those who follow the wheel of the year there will be some who don't celebrate set holidays or who celebrate holidays based on a different culture or paradigm. For every dozen who practice magic there may be one who sees it as superfluous to the witch's identity. To find one's place in modern witchcraft, ultimately, one must find one's own definition for what witchcraft is and how it is expressed and then seek to find the beliefs and practices most in line with that.

Modern witchcraft is a beautiful and fulfilling practice for those who choose to follow it and because it has so many different possible expressions there is a form of modern witchcraft to suit almost anyone. This has been just a small taste of what modern witchcraft is and can be in the world today, a quick overview of the larger things that can connect the wider community together. Beyond this, though, each separate tradition and approach is worth learning about and considering because each adds something of value to witchcraft both as a practice and religion. As you read further into this book, hopefully you will begin to discover some of the possibilities that exist within modern witchcraft and, if you feel witchcraft calls to you, find one particular approach that resonates with you.

Modern Solitary Witchcraft

Annette George

Modern witchcraft seems like a contradiction in terms. Witchcraft sounds ancient, something from our dark past, to be whispered about or spun into ghost stories on cold winters' nights. As I write this in the middle of October the shops are full of scary masks, fake blood, ghosts, ghouls, pumpkins and of course witches. Pointy hats, fake brooms and black dresses covered in sparkly cobwebs are standard uniform for a fashion conscious witch. In this, the twenty-first century we know all about witches, don't we? I mean we know everything about anything, with the Internet in the palm of our hands at home or in the middle of a field, we have access to information day and night. So finding out all we need to know about witches is child's play! Yet even now, the stereo typical witch is still portrayed as a gnarled old woman with a hooked nose, a penchant for drab dark clothing, with a feline or two in tow. I'm not sure if this is a blessing or a curse.

When I started on my path as a Pagan and a solitary witch I was amazed by the plethora of reading material available in the local bookstore. No longer hidden away under the counter, these books were brazen in their bright colors and tempting covers. I was slightly self-conscious when I took my chosen tome to the till to pay, thinking I'd be judged or there would be a shocked sharp intake of breath, or that the cashiers would franticly cross themselves. However, mine didn't blink an eyelid, I was out on the street clasping the book to my chest and I hadn't even been stoned or tied to a stake and burnt!

So I guess prejudging goes both ways. I expected the shoppers in the queue and the cashier to react to me in a certain way, and I was pleasantly surprised. I could come out of the broom cupboard, hooray!

Little did I realize at that point, I was about to enter a period of eye popping, purse busting pagan overload. As I read my newly purchased portal into the pagan world I soon found my stride, and wanted to self-initiate, set up an altar and start a Book of Shadows immediately! And of course, I couldn't wait to do these things, I wanted instant gratification. But where was I to obtain the tools to do all these magical things? The Internet came to my rescue (it being technologic witchery). Only I didn't realize what a mammoth task I had set myself. It's truly addictive, and costly if you're not careful. Herbs harvested from the other side of the world, crystals, incense, and spells, all readily available, twenty-four-seven. I was overwhelmed and lost myself in cyber shopping. Whilst it is wonderful to be able to get anything at any time, I found I had lost sight of why I was walking my path. I wanted to connect with nature and the seasons, yet how was I doing this buying all my equipment or ingredients online?

So after an initial gorging on the Internet I took a step back for a while. I bought several more books on witchcraft, and it was about then I discovered that what I thought was an ancient belief system was mostly a modern religion, developed and written about by Gerald Gardener in the 1950s. I was quite shocked to find a little white-haired, well to do nudist had exposed the rituals and spell work of a band of witches, and that is where Wicca had its roots. It wasn't quite what I had expected.

And slowly it dawned on me, that what I felt and what I believed could not be found in books, but it was within me. I didn't want someone telling me to do things this way or that way. We humans are blessed with being unique, and so to me, my journey should be and would be unique. It may follow other paths for a while, or cross others, but it was mine and mine alone to walk.

And so, taking baby steps, I spent time outside, connecting with the land around me: the woods, the streams, the mountains and the sea. I made my own wand, with a little help, (well most of it), from my husband. Though my first wand was a piece of wood that I picked up on a walk. And when I returned home I realized I still had it firmly in my hand. I knew then it had chosen me. In a similar vein my home altar is a muddle of items that have found their way back to the cottage. Sometimes it's a stone, a feather or a sea shell. Other times it's from a car boot or a charity shop. Preloved items are some of my most treasured, they have a history or a character of their own, a story to tell.

As a solitary witch, with no ancestral teaching, or coven to assist my journey I did find the Internet a doorway to connect, if and when I wanted to, with other pagans and witches. It was both a comfort and a source of conflict at my fingertips. I could be as anonymous or as public as I wished to be. Again something that could easily suck you in and devour you. I was amazed at how many websites and blogs there were. There was advice from all walks of the pagan path. But not only were others discussing their journey, but they were a wealth of information. The exact dates and times (to the second) of Sabbats were available instantly, and the moon phases there precisely. With busy lifestyles it was perfect for those who had so much to remember already. Not only were there websites for the busy pagan, but phone apps too!

From caldrons to tarot cards, witchcraft, is big business. Because there is an interest in "new age" religions or spiritual paths, it is now easier to earn a living from your path, or gift, as many do. Card readings, spells, potions, charms and amulets, and courses teaching others about various aspects of any chosen pagan belief are freely advertised on Ebay, Etsy and Facebook. YouTube is full of pagan Vloggers supplying videos on every aspect of witchcraft from how to set up your altar to how to cast a circle. Some of the videos are informative, and others fun, but I'm sure you'll find a video on there to answer most questions you'll have.

How blessed we are to live in an age of such tolerance and such acceptance. Though, there are still those out there, who are willing to persecute and discredit witches for their "dealings with the devil." I've experienced this modern-day witch hunt firsthand. It was via my Facebook page, "Highland Hedgewitch," I received vile messages and taunts of how I would rot in hell for my wicked ways. It got to a point where I changed the name of the page, I cut back any posts about paganism and basically tucked myself back into the dark safety of my broom cupboard. Then the words of a friend came to mind, she told me that if I was wanting to be happy with my beliefs, to inspire others, to educate them, then one of the first things I needed to do, before self-initiation or altar erecting, was to accept that once I stuck my head above the parapet and let the world see me as a witch, I should be ready and able to defend my choice. She said this was because someone was sure to take a shot at me. And what had I done? I had raced back and cowed at their nasty, petty words. Empowered by friends, and the thoughts of all those who had walked the path before, those who had been accused, persecuted and tortured for their beliefs, I went back to my page and stood up for my rights, and the rights of anybody else, to be whoever, and whatever they chose to be. Though it doesn't take much digging to discover that real life witch hunting still goes on in some countries such as Africa and India. I was shocked to read how even young children can be targeted and driven from their homes or worse, accused with little or no proof of any wrongdoing.

Living in the Highlands of Scotland I'm blessed with not only the right to be a witch, but also with an abundance of space in which to work. I do have close neighbors but I ensure that what I do has no impact on either the space or the people around me. Although surrounded by nature, I am also its prisoner. The weather is not conducive to outside rituals most of the year. If you're not being soaked in the rain, stung by freezing hail, you're being frozen by snow or flung about by gales. And if that isn't enough, you're eaten alive by the blight of the Highlands, the fearsome midge. Yet another bonus of solitary practice, I can adapt at a moment's notice and make use of the indoor space. With witchcraft, like many religions, you can choose to celebrate in a grandiose manner or it can be as simple as a silent prayer or words said over the preparation of a meal for loved ones.

I tend to keep things simple in my spell work and Sabbat celebrations, a large part of that is down to cost, but also a desire to keep things easy to remember and work with. Being on medication for various health reasons, I find my memory is not what it once was, hence the need for simplicity. One of my favorite ways to work magic is with candles, or with my open fire. There are not many days when my fire is not lit, mainly again due to the weather and the fact I live in an old cottage with thick stone walls, cold in both summer and winter. I have an altar in my kitchen window, where I spend a lot of time, or I walk past several times a day. The hearth in the living room is also a place I spend plenty of time, it is the heart of the home and so important to me. I use both these places to display crystals, incense or deities. My family is patient with me, and although they are not religious, they join me in Sabbat celebrations, or in certain spells. My husband helped me when I made a Hexenspiegel, a protective mirrored sphere to hang in the window to repel negativity, or dark magic. As it was to protect our home, he felt comfortable in performing the spell with me. I have a familiar, my cat Roxy, she is a feisty tiny tabby. She loves nothing more than to help me with my Tarot or Oracle cards, and routinely sits and watches, and has even selected cards before. However, she can also send them flying to the floor should she wish, and one or two bear her teeth marks! As a familiar she has no respect for the tools of my trade, especially crystals which she will chase if she can get them on the floor. She's not fond of incense, but will tolerate it when in the mood. She will also bring in a blood sacrifice. She was a house cat until quite recently, yet now when she catches a mouse or a bird she will bring it in and leave it by me, never eating it or chewing it. I always take the poor creatures to the garden, and say a few words as I return them to Mother Earth.

I mentioned my Oracle Cards and Tarot Cards. I have several decks, and have recently started a course on Angel Card reading. I believe in Angels as spiritual beings. As a witch some think that strange, but as a modern solitary it is one of the freedoms I find so appealing that I can choose what I believe in and no one can tell me it's right or wrong.

I choose to abide by "If it harm none, so mote it be," the Rule of Three, what you send out is returned to you three times as strong. So if you send out the good stuff that's great, but should you choose to dabble in the darker side of witchcraft, then you do so at your own risk. However, there are some who think that we should embrace the dark side of ourselves, as it is also part of who we are. That is a decision that has to be made on a personal level, and I wish you well with it. I have been asked many times for spells of a more destructive nature. It is not something I am comfortable with. Like love potions, if it goes against another's free will, it's not something I could agree to. But there are some who are more progressive and experimental than myself.

Being a modern witch, my deities also reflect this. Mainly due to availability of information about Gods and Goddesses from other parts of the world; I am not limited to just the local deities. Plus, I don't feel restricted to Wiccan deities. For instance, I love Jesus, as a spiritual teacher, and healer. Green Tara, Brigid and Hecate are also on my spiritual A-Team along with Archangels Michael and Metatron.

I love the fact that as a twenty-first-century solitary witch I can pick and choose what I do and when I do it. I can be as thoroughly modern as I wish, or as traditional as my mood takes me. I can use technology to aid my witchcraft with my online updated calendar, my Book of Shadows and my suppliers all in the palm of my hand accessible to me 24/7, in one device!

I wonder what the witches, pagans, cunning folk and wise men and women would have made of the world we have access to today. I'm sure they'd have seen the Internet as a form of magic. But the greatest of all magic achieved over the past few hundred years is that I can stand up today, free of fear of persecution for myself and my family, and declare that I am a witch.

Modern Witchcraft & the Role of Activism

Irisanya Moon

> Because everything is interdependent, there are no simple, single causes and effects. Every action creates not just an equal and opposite reaction, but a web of reverberating consequences.
> Starhawk, *The Earth Path: Grounding Your Spirit in the Rhythms of Nature*

We live in dangerous, confusing times. No matter where you are reading this, we continue to live in times that challenge, that inspire, that call out to us to take action. As Witches, as magick-makers, we often say that "what happens between the worlds changes all the world." When we step into magickal space, when we step into the place between, we have a responsibility to step up for the earth and for each other.

And we don't do this work alone.

Whether one's witchcraft looks like celebrating the seasons or marching on the streets, there is a responsibility to take care of the Earth and her inhabitants. If we are to be stewards of the land and protectors of beings, we are activists – even if it looks different from person to person.

> [P]ersonal problems are political problems. There are no personal solutions at this time. There is only collective action for a collective solution.
> Carol Hanisch, *The Personal is Political*

We can see in nature the results of our actions and the way each decision we make impacts another. Though we will not see all of the results of our choices, as Witches, we understand we have a

16

role to play.

That said, it can certainly be overwhelming to know where to begin. With the structures of oppression in place, with the intersectional nature of our personal experiences, we can often see more problems than solutions. We see more questions than answers.

As Witches, we can start with the personal issues that impact us directly each day. Whether we are the direct or indirect victims of patriarchy, of racism, of environmental destruction, of gentrification, etc., we see a list of places to work our magick and to create conditions of change and freedom.

Reclaiming's roots dive deep into the dismantling of structures of oppression. We seek to create a tradition and a culture of non-hierarchy, of consensus, of social justice, and of continuing questioning of how we can uncover internalized oppression. And we do not do this work alone.

Political actions

In 2017 on October 31, Hex for the Future began in the Civic Center Plaza in San Francisco.

The ritual-art-activist event was opened by three Two Spirit indigenous people, including Kanyon Sáyres-Roods, a local Mutsun Ohlone from Indian Canyon Nation. The "witchcraft" at this event was real and beautiful, but it wasn't a single community of people. Some came as self-identified witches linked to various pagan and indigenous communities. Some dressed up as witches for Halloween and enjoyed the camp and activist aspects of the event. Five of the 12 "lead witches" are Two Spirit native people.

(Hex was instigated by Keith Hennessy and Annie Danger, managed by Circo Zero, and supported by SF Arts Commission and California Arts Council.)

The group marched to City Hall to "open the gates to a just future and a broad, deep, liberated political imagination: Free of prisons and jails. Free of police. Reparations. Housing for all. Justice for the ancestors and the children and us all. True sanctuary. Power to the people."

Four red banners were spread down the steps of City Hall, naming the spell's intentions: Housing, Abolition, Reparations, and Sanctuary.

The witches gathered and the spell was cast.

From protesting the WTO to supporting Standing Rock to marching against the current political systems, many Witches (not just Reclaiming) have stood up to gather energy. In the gathering of intentions and bodies, Witches begin to tear down webs of lies, shatter mirrors of illusion, and welcome a world of justice.

Drums play, chants begin, songs flood the spaces to call out to the Gods for help, for guidance, for change. Together, Witches march and link arms and perform ritual dramas to call attention to the places of peril, to bring into light that which has been hidden, and to call out to others to join the fight.

We can cast circles of protection around us as we walk in the streets. We can model non-hierarchical interactions as we plan, as we move, and as we decide what to do next. We can leave space for all voices, and lift up the voices that often go unheard.

Ritual

In communities, public ritual becomes the place where activism emerges alongside the cycles of the Earth. At Brigid (which some know as Imbolc), there is a long-standing spell in Reclaiming to promote the freedom of the waters and to call for clean waters for all people. By taking waters from different areas of the land, the ritual participants add their own watershed and water source names. The waters are charged and people can take back these Waters of the World to continue the spell across the years.

At Beltane, the celebration of sexuality and fertility in all of its forms is the magical act of reclaiming our birthright as humans. By calling out and dancing around the May Pole, we can invite into the world the opportunities for all genders, all sexualities, and all sexual histories to be free to know pleasure, to release shame and stories, and to build the energy that is sent out into the world to those who may not have the same freedom.

At the equinoxes, we consider the balance and the tipping point. We often consider what has become out of balance in the land and in ourselves. We look to the shift into light and shadow as an invitation to consider what can be changed.

At the solstices, those longest and shortest days, we step back into the times when it was unclear whether the light would return or the night would come. We embrace the metaphors of times of unknowing and hope. We come together to share in the wisdom of ourselves, of the stories of tension and confusion. And we can remember the presence of cycles and the memory of that which leaves can return again.

At Lammas, we remember the places of our harvest, and the seeds we've planted. The things we've grown and the things we've let die. We often gather in a shared meal, where we can remember the blessings that started as seeds, and we can begin to consider how we might prepare for times when things may not be as bountiful.

During Samhain, we remember our dead, the ones who have been here before, the ones who can see beyond our present moment and who can see back into where we have been. We call out to the ancestors, the descendants, the Beloved Dead, and our Mighty Dead to share their wisdom. To answer the questions, we ask about how we can create change in the world. We can remember that we are not alone in our questioning, and we are supported on all sides. We can even remember that our ancestors lead us and the descendants follow us as we make the choices we make.

We can work with the moon, the growing and shrinking. What are the things we want to grow in the world? What do we want to release or diminish? What are the ways we can work with the cycles of time or growth to align with the changes we wish to see?

And there are other opportunities to call out the injustices of the world, to bring them into ritual where we can trance into our experiences, we can connect with others who feel lost, and we can sink into our inner knowing so that we might be able to know what to do next. We might come together in ritual to call out the secrets of oppression, to grieve for those who have been killed because of oppression, and to renew ourselves so that we may continue to fight.

Becoming activists

The truth is that whatever we do as Witches, we will have an impact. And we also have a responsibility. We are activists merely in the fact that we choose to go outside of the overculture to know magick as real.

But not everyone clings to that name or title as something they are. For not all activists look the same. Not everyone is able or willing or excited about getting on the frontline of a political action with the potential of getting themselves arrested. Not everyone is physically able to march or to spend hours on the phone talking to their representatives.

This is okay. Just as there are a hundred ways to kneel and kiss the ground, there are hundreds of ways to be an activist. There is space for all.

Know what calls to you – If the pull of creating change in the world is enticing, then the best way to begin is to think about what stirs your blood. What are the issues that most resonate with you? Sexism? Racism? Abortion rights? Environmental causes? When you can choose an issue that speaks to you, you will find the energy to take steps to support it. And the reality is that you cannot change everything all on your own. Stand up for the things that matter most to you, stand up for the people that need you.

Find allies – Once you know what you want to engage in, find others who share in your passion. There are many groups and organizations that you can step into and that you can support. Do the research to find out who you can call allies, who will stand by your side in the steps you take today and tomorrow. Even amongst your friends, find a circle of support that you can turn to when things seem bleak or confusing or exciting.

Take small steps – You may not have a lot of time or resources to do all that you want to do, so make a list of the things you can do. Not sure where to start? Ask your allies. Ask the groups you participate in. Make a list of the things you can do and start crossing them off. Each little step may not seem to have direct results, but when many take small steps, they begin a movement.

Refill your cup – A common concern with activism in all of its forms is burnout. Make sure that as you begin to take action for others that you also take care of yourself. Make time for self-care and rest. You don't have to show up all the time for everything that's happening. You can choose to do some things and then focus on yourself. When you honor your abilities and your energy, you will be able to stay engaged more often. And you will model this practice for others.

Create ritual – When you see something that needs to be highlighted, create a ritual for chance. You might create it with your coven or a local group, or just with yourself. Develop an intention that speaks to the thing you see and what it means to you. You might create a ritual that seeks to expose the lies in the world. This might include creating sacred space and then exploring the lies that have been told. You might have participants call out those lies and scream them into the sky. You might then take the energy of these lies and seek to alchemize it by singing a song of hope and possibility. Move the energy so that it is not stuck in the places it was. Continue to sing and to dance and to drum until the shift happens. Even if the power structures don't fall in that very moment, realize that as a group (and even as an individual), you have ignited the possibility of change. You have opened up inspiration and determination for whatever steps need to happen next.

Attend events – Over time, seek out events where you can be supportive to others. This work is not something that you do alone all the time. You need other people, you need other Witches to remind you of what you're fighting for.

The future

No matter what moment of time you're in right now, look forward. No matter what problems you're facing personally or collectively, move forward. You are not the first person who sees the world as filled with problems. And you can be the person who sees the world as filled with potential.

Modern witchcraft and activism are a good fit. Witchcraft is a reminder of things that are bigger than us and activism calls out our names as those who can be forces of change, there is no better time to begin than now.

We can use our tools of raising energy to bring energy to the things we want to call into the world. We can call to the Gods and their stories to find inspiration to rewrite narratives and find ourselves as heroes and heroines

We can use hexes and spell work to bring into being new dynamics, more clarity, and thwarted injustices. We can call on each other in the circle to step in as allies and as co-conspirators in change.

We can sing songs that light the way and that empower us to speak up when our voices shake. We can make promises in sacred space to do more, to do better. We can blend the herbs and the potions to fuel inner strength and to release the tension of the fight.

As modern Witches, we can use social media to focus our intentions, to call out what we see, and to model being truth-tellers. We can hold ourselves accountable through the process of learning and unlearning our own limitations.

We can love each other and trust each other perfectly and imperfectly.

We can be activists in all that we do. The time is now.

Urban Witchcraft

Rebecca Beattie

A few years ago, I was babysitting a friend's Occult Bookshop – Treadwells, in London. A young seeker came into the shop and began browsing around the shop. Each new treasure she found caused her eyes to open up, just a little bit wider, and I could see her head was full of questions. Finally, as she reached the Witchcraft shelf, she couldn't contain herself any longer. Turning to me, she bubbled over completely.

"Do you believe in witches?" She asked, and with barely a pause for breath, "Are you a witch?"

I probably looked like a startled rabbit while I tried to compose my thoughts. I come from a line of Gardnerian witches. If you are in the States you may see it referred to on Internet forums as BTW – British Traditional Witchcraft – but in the UK we just think of ourselves as Wiccan, or witches. Our tradition is oath bound, so in most situations if someone asks a question, Wiccans will give a vague answer, demur, or very artfully change the topic as quickly as possible, particularly if they are not "out" in public. However, when faced with this particular seeker, on this particular day, I had two problems. Firstly, I was sitting behind the counter in an occult bookshop which meant I couldn't deny all knowledge, and secondly, when I am asked a direct question, I have an inability to lie. This does not mean I will spill all of my oath-bound-beans to any old Tom, Dick or Harriet, but on this occasion I replied, that yes, I believe in witches, and yes, I am one. And the question that came up next floored me even more.

"How can you practice witchcraft when you live in the city?" she asked, "I thought witches had to live in the countryside."

This is a question that often echoes in my mind, and I often return to it in my writing. Although I grew up in a very remote part of Dartmoor, I have lived in London for nearly twenty years now, and have a very rich and varied spiritual path, even though I am living in such urban surroundings, and practicing a nature-based faith. So, for those of you who may be simply curious, or those of you struggling to find your way in similar circumstances, in this chapter I want to unpick some of the elements at play in successfully practicing Urban Witchcraft. I don't think that young seeker was alone in thinking that in order to be a "proper witch" we must live in a cottage on the edge of a wood somewhere like Granny Weatherwax, and while that might be appealing for all sorts of reasons, the economic realities of living in contemporary society often mean that this is a dream that is not possible for many of us to manifest.

You may be tethered to the city because of work, or study, or family members. Or you may simply feel all at sea in a truly rural setting. Some people feel less safe in the wilder lands where there are less people around. Growing up on Dartmoor, but being drawn to live in our capital city, I had to go through a process of learning to find peace here. So, in the hopes that it may help you along, and enable you to find some peace amidst all the dust and noise, here are some of the tricks I have learned over the years for practicing Urban Witchcraft. Some of them may seem obvious, and many of them could apply to rural Witchcraft as well as urban, but this is really a reminder to apply the same principles in an urban setting.

Find Nature

It may seem obvious to some of you, but the first essential in practicing Urban Witchcraft is in finding nature. Even in the most urban parts of the city, nature is always around us; sometimes you just need to look differently to find it. For instance, London is blessed with a plethora of trees that line every pavement, but often the leaf canopy is higher than we are, and we may forget to look up and see the green. One of the offices I worked in was on the fourth floor of a building, which gave me the perfect vantage point. If I looked out of the window I was sitting right in amongst the leaves. Working higher up also gave me a spectacular vantage point for some of the most glorious skyscapes I have ever seen. Make a point of observing your surroundings as much as possible, and make sure you are really looking at the details.

Closer to the ground, if you pay attention to what's around your feet, you will also get some surprises. The grass verges that line the main road I live on are clustered with tiny outbreaks of wild chamomile. Map out your local area and make sure you know where things are – the elderflower tree that grows round the corner, the rosemary bushes that profuse the local park, the place where you can safely gather fresh nettles, away from the pollution of the busy roads that criss-cross the land we live in.

While city parks also allow for some very special close encounters with nature and wildlife (I have come closer to herons and foxes in the centre of London than I did on Dartmoor) there are also areas of green belt that rove around the outer edges of the city. If you need to find these spaces, you can scout out footpaths by checking the website of your local authority for local walking information.

There will be footpaths and woodlands and wilder places there somewhere, usually on the outskirts and the edgelands, or near rivers and canals. Go there as often as you can, and just watch the turning of the seasons. See what is in bloom, and when, and get to know the land as if it is another one of your companions. The city is full of history and soul, and there are lots of ways to connect with it, even if it is tightly wrapped in tarmac, and hedged in with wire fences.

Your area may be choked in litter, but there may also be schemes you can volunteer with to improve the environment. Perhaps the estate you live on has a neighborhood scheme for conservation? If so, volunteer! It is an act of service to your home that will help deepen your ties.

Finding Solitude

This one is harder to do than finding nature, but it is not impossible. One of the elements of Dartmoor that I miss more than anything is the solitude. If you are an extrovert and recharge by being in the company of others, then you are already pre-set for city life. If, like me, you need peace and quiet, then there are a few ways of finding it. When I worked in Central London, each time I was in rush hour or out in the street at lunch times, I felt like I was going to get swallowed up or run over by the crowd. The vast numbers of people, all moving in a certain direction and not pausing to let anyone through was quite intimidating. So I learned to find the back streets and the quiet spaces. If I am walking, I will make a point of moving at my own pace, to make sure I am fully mindful and present in what I am doing in that moment. That is how you spot the details of nature around you.

Another element to finding solitude is to walk at times when most people are still tucked up in their beds. I walk as early in the morning as I can, as I encounter less people and more wildlife then. Also, it is much easier to connect to the Divine in solitude. The gods – in whatever form you relate to them – are communicating with us all the time, through nature and through your own inner voice – that quiet voice you can only hear when you make yourself still and allow it to speak. That is why we need the peace and quiet, to see the signs that are all around us, and to hear our own inner prompting.

Embracing Your Inner Weirdo

I once said to my husband that I was worried about meeting strange people in the woods, he laughed and said, "Don't worry – you *are* the strange people in the woods!"

In some ways he is absolutely right. Witches tend to live on the outskirts of society, whether we mean to or not. We are the outcasts, the odd-bods, the weirdos. We are the ones that get caught, turning over a leaf on the tree to see the color of its underside, or picking up pebbles in the park, or gathering fresh nettles in the patch of waste ground that sits just up the alleyway. Embrace your inner nerd, and don't worry too much what other people think. You might think you are projecting a good impression of "normal," but normal is a myth, like unicorns or the phoenix. Just embrace being yourself and let everyone else worry about what they think or don't think about that. Our whole purpose in life is to be as authentically ourselves as we can, and you can't do that if you are busy worrying about what people think of you.

Find the Sacred Spaces

When you are scouting your local neighborhood for pockets of nature, it's also a good idea to scope out where the sacred sites are. If I am in the city, I am not averse to visiting other people's sacred sites for an encounter with the divine, and I know I am not alone. People I know of all different faiths sometimes do likewise. It is not uncommon for churches or temples to be built on top of older sacred sites. For instance, St. Paul's Cathedral in London was once the site of a temple to Isis, while the temple in Luxor (Egypt) has a Mosque built on top of a church, on top of a temple. Sacred sites can be a magical experience whatever your faith. As one of my friends was fond of telling me, "same bush, different way round it." If you don't have a city park near your workplace, and you need some sacred space, then visit the local church instead. Use the spaces around you as a place of peace, and find that place of connection where you can.

Find Your Tribe

You might think the best aspect to urban living is the ease with which you can build social circles, but life in the city can be quite lonesome. We often live a distance away from the people we work with, and finding your tribe – that is, those like-minded people you can bond with and form a social group with – can be challenging. Recent studies have shown there is an undeniable link between lack of emotional connections and addictions or addictive behavior, so, scientists are only just beginning to grasp just how vital those love connections are. This means that building your social group is really important.

But how do you find it in the city? Usually by doing the things you love to do, so start getting out there – by signing up for classes at your local occult bookshop, or by attending talks and open rituals. Find the space that feels safe to you, and build your connections. Don't be disheartened if you don't have instant results – trust bonds take time to develop, but they will come. And before you know it, you will look around you and realize you have built yourself a very fine practice of Urban Witchcraft.

CyberWitch: Witchcraft in the Cyber Age

Philipp J. Kessler

I grew up in the early days of computers in the household. I was eight years old when the first Commodore-64 came into our home. That was 1986. I've been a part of the online community longer than many of the new Witches out there have been alive; I was using the Internet before it was open to the general public. I don't claim to be an expert on being a CyberWitch, but I can certainly claim having a history with the technology and how it can and does work with witchcraft.

A brief history ...

"Lay your hands on the holy modem and intone the sacred numerals ..." Those or similar words were jokingly said by many modemers in the late 1980s and early 1990s. They were the opening words to a spell of communication. Back in the days of CompuServe and AOL, before Facebook, Twitter, Pinterest, and other social media platforms, witches and Pagans, practitioners of the ancient and new arts of magick, were flocking to dial-up one node systems and IRCs.

For many of our Witch forebears in the late twentieth century, technology was where they hid. Sure, you had your farmers and ranchers, your small town Witches and even your urban Witches. But it was through technology that they began to connect. In the early days of the modern Witchcraft movement, it was through one sheets, newsletters, and even early magazines of the community that many Witches were able to connect. We still have some of those around today, but many of them have moved into the Cyber Age with websites, Tumblr, and Facebook pages.

Somewhere in the middle, between the snail mail newsletters and correspondence courses and the social media networks we had the listservs and other e-groups. It was around that time that I stumbled into the world of Witchcraft outside of books and magazines. With SIGs (special interest groups) on dial-up systems and the existence of eGroups and Yahoo!Groups, it was inevitable that we would eventually learn of Witches and Pagans using technology to spread their teachings, practices, and even take on students. Not to mention practice our magickal arts through modern tech.

I was declared a heretic by Queen Zanoni of the Georgian Tradition of Wicca in the late 1990s because I was willing and able to use the Internet to communicate and teach long distance students. It wasn't until years later that I found I was in good company, Dorothy Morrison having been declared a heretic by the same HPS of the Georgians. Zanoni has since changed her tune and used web videos to share her experiences and help preserve the history of the Craft. (The Keepers of the Flame video series interviewed her in the early 2010s.)

Many assume that using the Internet to teach magick and witchcraft is anathema to the ideals of the culture surrounding both the art of magick and the spirituality of Paganism. As we can see by looking at the early history of the modern movements, separate yet connected, they have used whatever means are available to them to connect and to learn from each other. The use of computers and the Internet is a logical evolution of the Craft of the Witch and of the Wise.

Hundreds, even thousands, of Witches connect over Facebook and other social media on a daily basis. They converge in discussion groups and chat rooms across the Internet to share their experiences and learn from each other. Projects like Magical Experiments, started by Taylor Ellwood, and the works of Eric Vernor and Bill Duvendack have opened the doors (or should I say portals) to real and effective magical training via the Internet. Many of these online training schools are open to new students. They do have strenuous qualifiers before they take you on for training. (The list of online teaching schools is boundless, I name these few as ones that I am familiar with directly.)

Likewise, there are dozens of Witchcraft schools and academies directly associated with various Pagan or Wiccan traditions. Black Rose Academy, the Grey School of Witchcraft and the Temple of Witchcraft come to mind, as well as the distance training of the Correllian Tradition. These academies have students hundreds, even thousands, of miles away from their parent groups and regularly scheduled events in which the students and teachers can meet in person and be granted their magickal degrees and titles.

What is a CyberWitch?

The Craft is not a system of dogmas and mere beliefs. It is a way of becoming more of what we can and should be.

Victor Anderson, founder of the Feri Tradition of Witchcraft

The talk of technomages and cyber-craft has been around as long as computers have been accessible to your average person. Maybe before even.

William Gibson, author of *Neuromancer* (1984) and many other books in the cyber sci-fi genre, gave us the term cyberspace. J. Michael Straczynski in 1991 gave us the *Babylon 5* TV series, including a faction of mages known as Techno Mages. Combining the two, we have what some might call CyberWitches in the world of science fiction.

It is but a simple step into reality to take the ideas presented by these two sci-fi masterminds and come to what is in fact a form of Cyber Witchcraft. We are not yet wet-wired into the Matrix, but we are a breath away from being able to embrace the idea of using technology and science to continue, and to grow, our practices. Many have already done so ...

A CyberWitch, to me, is someone who uses the technology at

hand to further their magickal practice. They are not a person who limits themselves by what they already know. That can be said for most Witches. We tend to use what we can find and learn how to use new things as we encounter them. A CyberWitch will also take the idea, the inkling of an idea, and run with it. Can a computer be used in ritual? Can an mp3 player cast a Circle of Protection? Can you store your grimoire on a thumb drive?

The answer to those questions, and more like them, is a resounding YES.

Yes, you can use your computer in ritual. Several Witchcraft traditions have been known to gather in the cyber world – from around the globe – to celebrate Sabbats and Esbats or other holy days. Skype and other VOIP (voice over Internet phone) applications can be used to do this. Or, you can just log into your Facebook and perform a ritual in a group or on a page. I'd be really surprised if no one has used the Facebook Live feature to lead a ritual or guided meditation. Hellenion.org conducts their classes, rituals, etc. almost exclusively online.

Yes, you can use your mp3 player to create sacred space. My own tradition, the Covenant of Kernunnos, has used mp3 players or other digital media players to cast Circle and create the space. You can even use the player itself as the wand or athame!

Yes, you can use a thumb drive or other digital storage device for your grimoire. Back in the 1990s Sapphire published her Book of Shadows on CD-ROM. I, somehow, have several copies of that disc in my library.

Do all of these digital or cyber technologies negate or lessen the value? Hardly! Some might say so, and for them that is true. But for the rest of us, those who are willing to explore the cyber realms, they are of equal value to the Old Ways of face-to-face ritual, playing an instrument in Circle, or scratching your spells onto parchment with quill and ink. It all works. Just depends on what you are willing to try.

Experimentation

What does it take to be a CyberWitch? Experimentation is the key. It is the key to almost all acts of Witchcraft and magick when you boil it down. A CyberWitch has to experiment in different ways. They have to be willing to take the chance on technology. We've all heard how technology and magick don't work well together. That is a mindset that has been in the way of many a CyberWitch or TechnoMage being able to do what they know they can do. Each Witch or Mage knows that s/he can cast a Circle, a spell, or otherwise create something magickal. They know it instinctually. But when you mix tech in with the magick, many of them panic.

Is this going to work? Am I really going to be able to cast a spell over the Internet? Can I do this (insert magickal thing)?

Of course it is going to work! Of course you can cast a spell over the Internet! That magickal thing will work! Might not work the way you think it will, at least not at first. You've got to allow for lag and for the programming language to translate. (See what I did there?) You might need a piece of rose or clear quartz on your computer or hanging off your mobile device to clear up any glitches, but it will work. I assure you.

Spell work, casting a Circle, and doing magick in general is using energy. Technology, the cyber world, runs on energy. Electricity, is one of the most basic and little understood elements of energy. We ourselves are little more than a condensed mass of rapidly vibrating electrons – electricity. Your athame or wand, your Tarot cards, and everything else you use to do magick, are all condensed electrons. The planet beneath your feet, the water in the ocean, the tree in your front yard are all dense piles of electricity. The fire that warms your hearth is less dense, but it still electricity – energy. The light of the stars and the visible form of the planets are all energy. Your thoughts are energy.

What does this all mean? Everything you do, from taking that first sip of coffee in the morning to your last bite of a midnight snack, from breathing to talking. It is all energy. What does the Internet hold? Millions and trillions of tiny bytes of energy that have been encoded with some programming language or another to hold information, pictures, videos, words. It is all energy. Magick is the manipulation of energy. A programming language is the manipulation of energy. The words we speak and write are manipulations of energy.

Imagine, if you will, that saying a spell out loud is the same as typing it into your keyboard. If you put the intent in the magick, both spells work. If you design a ritual on your computer's word processing program, you can create that ritual design in your own imagination. You had to in order to put it on the screen. Right? Take that one step further. The ritual design is there on your computer, you have shared it with those who are participating in the ritual. Everyone puts their intent and their energy into making it a reality. It is real.

Let's look at it another way. Have you been asked to light a candle for someone's health or a pet's journey over the rainbow bridge? Many of us have. Let's assume you are one of that many. Did you do it? Was the person miles away? Probably. But you did it anyway, right? Lighting a candle for someone's health or a pet's crossing is something that a lot of us do for our friends and loved ones. We don't even think about whether it will work. It just does. We are sending blessings and healing through the air, through space, to those who need it. Many of us have done something similar with ritual work – raising energy for a specific purpose and releasing and directing it into the air above us, into space. You can do the very same thing, with varying degrees of success, by lighting a virtual candle or typing a prayer or spell into an email. You are focusing that energy, that intent, into what you are doing and releasing it or directing it to where it is needed.

Using technology to do spell work and magick is not that different from doing it physically. The digital world has brought us into a new realm. Not a new plane of existence, but closer to understanding just how close we are to the invisible world.

To boldly go where no Witch has gone before ...

Witchcraft challenges us to do better, to be more, to go further. To paraphrase Gene Roddenberry, one of the fathers of modern science fiction, we are challenged to boldly go where no Witch has gone before. Take a chance on technology if you haven't already. It is a great resource for your magickal workings. You don't have to set up your next Beltane ritual on Skype or even share your latest herbal recipe in a chatroom. You don't have to go somewhere you don't want to go, but I challenge you to take a risk and do something different with your technology and your magick.

Fire up the laptop and write out your next ritual – I'm sure many of you already do that. Then send it via email to your co-religionists for feedback. Maybe get together over Skype or some other VOIP to plan out who is going to do what or bring the cookies. Maybe even take a chance and do an oral run through on that next ritual. You might be surprised at what good it does.

Tap your next spell or recipe into your mobile phone or other device. Post it to Facebook if you feel like others can benefit from it. Share and grow in your Craft by using your tech. There are so many of us online, we can learn a lot from each other if we but take the time to explore and open ourselves to the new possibilities that the Cyber Age has brought to us.

Do something different with your tech. You just might be surprised at how powerful a CyberWitch or TechnoMage you can become!

Web Weaving for the Modern Witch

Amie Ravenson

I walk into my office, turn on the ceiling fan, and light a few candles. I pull a book on magickal herbalism from the shelf, and bring it to my desk. There, I light a stick of incense and more candles, and wake my computer from its slumber.

The monitor flashes on, and I'm greeted by a picture of the triple Goddess. I type in my password, unlocking access to the knowledge and connections that I'll be finding online tonight. I take a moment, look at the shrines to my deities here at my desk and say a silent prayer to them to help me find the magick that I seek.

I launch my browser, and a series of tabs come up with my favorite websites. There are seven, and three of them are social networks. I look through the others, first setting my Internet radio station, and then reading a few articles and blog posts. I find it's easier to do a little solitary browsing before I try to deal with people.

The truth is, I'm an introvert in real life. My little rituals and habits help me relax into socializing, even online. So I take a few minutes to ease into things.

When I'm finally ready, I check for comments on my videos and answer them. Making videos about tarot and my Pagan practice has opened my world to a whole new group of witches and Pagans. I've made some amazing friends here.

Then I go to one of the major social networks. This is where I tend to make the most connections. Here, I've met people from all over the world, mostly Pagans from all walks of life. Some are solitary like me, some are in covens. Some are authors like me, some are artists, parents, business people, farmers, and anything else you can imagine. As always, I feel a little thrill that the world is so filled with those of us that believe in and create magick wherever possible.

I make a post wishing everyone a happy full moon, and talk a little about my plans to celebrate it. Within minutes, I get comments back wishing me a happy full moon as well!

This is web weaving at its very finest. When I pluck a string with my typed words, it reverberates all over the web (both the "world wide web," and the metaphorical web of connection we share with everyone in the world). Sometimes those reverberations bring back joy and a deep sense of community. Sometimes we piss the wrong people off, and the reverberations bring us back antagonism or small-mindedness. But what we do counts, and the connections we make online give us clear and immediate examples of that.

So how do we find these connections and the magick they can bring into our lives? The short answer is that they're everywhere. You can start with social networks that you already belong to. There are dozens of Pagan groups on Facebook of varying quality and activity. Join several, and then weed out the ones you don't love. I've met some really amazing people on these groups, and I've also gotten involved in some drama as well. Just maintain a healthy respect for other group members, and a healthy awareness of the block button if they don't respect you in turn.

Twitter can also be a great way to meet other Pagans. I've had great luck just searching for hashtags, but the more specific the hashtag is, the better. For example, searching for #MabonRecipes is going to give you more immediate, targeted results than searching for #Pagan, which will bring back a wide array of things you may or may not be looking for. Once you've followed some Pagan tweeters, interact with them! Comment on their tweets, retweet the ones you love, and tweet about your practice. That way, people can find and follow you too, and that's when the conversations begin!

Pagan bloggers are everywhere nowadays too. As a Pagan blogger myself, I love nothing more than receiving a comment from someone who has read my blog posts and wants to start a discussion about something I said. If cruising all over the Internet to keep up with the blogs you want to follow isn't your thing, take a look at various apps that collect RSS feeds. You can do that by searching "RSS readers" in your app store. That way, you can add a blog as soon as you find it, and you can open the app to read blog posts from all of your favorite bloggers in one place. It's kind of like creating your own magickal newspaper. Don't forget to add other things you're interested in too. I read blogs on herbalism, astrology, tarot, vegan cooking, and various other things that all feed into my practice in one way or another.

If you find blog posts that speak to you, share it on other social media, and start conversations about it. Also, leave comments on the bloggers' posts, and let them know what you think. Any discussion you start could be a potential friendship down the line, so it's always worth telling someone that you love what they do, or offer suggestions of what you'd like to see them talk about.

Videos are an amazing way to learn about other people's practices. In fact, I probably watch more YouTube than TV these days. It's a great way to find very specific content about the very specific things I want to learn. I love it so much that I even started creating my own videos, and I encourage you to do the same! The community that has grown up around Pagan vloggers is quite strong, diverse, and friendly. It's really a great place to meet people and learn new things. I recommend searching for "Book of Shadows" or "Grimoire" to get started, as people love to talk about how they record their magickal experiences. If you make comments on videos, you're sure to find friends. Not only do people who put themselves "out there" love to get comments on their videos, but other fans are eager to talk about what they're watching too.

There are also various dedicated Pagan social networks floating around online. I've joined several of them, but haven't had great success. They have a tendency to fizzle after time, and they're heavily chat based. Personally, I don't do very well in a chat environment, as I'm better following one single thread, one train of thought. Your mileage may vary! Search "Pagan social network" or "Wiccan social network" and see what you find. If you love to chat, you may find a place to call home and help to keep it going.

So as you can see, you can really find Pagans anywhere online. I do recommend meeting people in person as well, like at open rituals in your area, local Pagan Pride events, even at your local metaphysical stores. But there are a lot of people who live in remote areas, or who live in environments that are hostile to their spiritual expression, so those may not be options for everyone. Meeting people online can sometimes be the best option. But what do we do with those connections once we find them?

There are so many ways to bring the friendships you make online into your life. You may find that you spend all night messaging someone that you have common interests and views with, even if they live hundreds or thousands of miles away. I've had some purely Internet-based friendships that have been closer than friendships with people I see all the time. It's amazing to find people that you can connect with so deeply.

If you love the idea of group work, but can't get out to visit local covens (or don't have any local covens around), you can start a search for online covens. They are everywhere! If you don't find one you like, talk to some of the Pagan friends you've met online and see if they want to start one. A great way to do this is to start a private Facebook group for just your coven, where you share posts about things you think everyone will enjoy, set up events for times to meet online, and set up a group chat in Messenger. A great way to "meet" is to use a group chat program with video capabilities for face-to-face discussions. This is a good way to do ritual together if you would like. Each person would just set up their own ritual space, and then log into a video chat. That way, you can see everyone's faces and hear their words as you do ritual in your own space. The power you can generate over distances in this way can be quite astonishing.

You can meet on the full moons, the new moons, every Friday, or five times a week if you'd like. The possibilities are endless, as long as you can find people with the same desire for community and the same level of engagement as you.

As with any other friendship or community, there is the possibility that your online connections will falter or fall apart. That's normal, and part of the experience of meeting people online. The truth is that there are so many of us floating around in the world, that we don't have to stick together if we aren't having fun. Before the Internet, Pagans met in tight, secret groups, and I think a lot of people compromised themselves and their practice just to find people to practice with. Now, we have so many options and so many people to meet that we can seek out the people who truly "get us" and lift us and our practice. If someone is difficult to work with, sees things drastically differently, or just generally drags you down, you can dismiss them with a thanks and wishes for you both to continue your paths separately but happily. The important thing to keep in mind is that the Internet is a great place to call forward that which feeds you, and to politely (or sometimes not so politely) dismiss that which drains you.

We also have a responsibility to examine what we're sending out into the world. With this "plucking of the strings of the web," we can choose to spread happiness and positivity, or we can choose to complain, whine, stir up trouble, or cause unhappiness. With the results of our interactions so clearly apparent and immediate, it gives us a unique opportunity to decide who we want to be in the world, and what we want to create and spread. Personally, I love to connect with people over creative pursuits like painting, poetry, writing, etc. I feel like part of my life path in this lifetime is to cheerlead people into following their creative bliss. I love to see how many people are embracing creative pursuits and sharing their work with the world. It makes me supremely happy, and feeds my spirituality.

What would you like to champion? What would you like to spread in the world? Connecting with Pagan folks online gives you that unique ability to create connections that will help you bring forth your vision and pursue your intended path. The important thing to remember is that there are dozens, if not hundreds of Pagan folks that are looking for someone just like you too!

Here are some ideas to get you started. You can search for Pagan parenting, Pagan cooking, Pagan celebrations, Pagan dating, Pagan music, Pagan artists, Pagan journaling prompts, various Pagan traditions (Norse, Celtic, Aztec, etc.), Pagan herbalism, spiritual travel, women's retreats, divination, astrology, stones and crystals, candle magick, chaos magick, local Pagan or Wiccan groups, Books of Shadows groups, or pretty much anything else you can think of. The more specific the group is, the more likely you are to find your people there.

As always, you can find me and friend me anywhere! I go by AmieRavenson across the board. Let's connect and build something wonderful together!

Kitchen Witchcraft: From Fire Pit to Fitted Kitchen Magic

Rachel Patterson

Those that have gone before, the ones with magic in their veins would have worked kitchen witchcraft as a matter of everyday life. They probably wouldn't have called it kitchen witchcraft; in fact they would not have really considered it witchcraft. It was the craft of the wild woman or man; it was wort cunning and healing with maybe the odd curse thrown in for good measure if a neighbor upset them.

Herbs, flowers and seeds would have been collected from the hedgerows and the fields and hung up to dry. Later to be transformed into poultices, tinctures and remedies. I think the kitchen witch and the hedge witch have a good deal of cross over, moving from the outside fire with the cooking pot suspended above it to the inside of an old cottage kitchen. Although both "titles" are fairly modern as far as I know.

But how does it carry over into modern-day life? Do I need a fire pit in the garden with a cauldron hanging above it or a kitchen ceiling hung with drying herbs? No is my answer to both of those questions. Like most things it has evolved and changed along with modern-day life. The fire pit has become the cooker and the cauldron the casserole dish. Whilst some do still hang herbs from the ceiling to dry, others purchase them already dried in convenient little pots from the supermarket and that is absolutely okay in fact it is more than okay.

Our modern-day connection to the kitchen has ebbed and flowed from the idea of the 1950s housewife spending most of her day doing the cleaning and creating home cooked meals for her husband to the 1970s when "ready meals" and frozen food emerged. Then the 1980s (my favorite decade for fashion and music ... don't judge) when very pretty but tiny food appeared on our plates through to now. We can purchase any kind of food whether it is in season or not. Dishes from around the world fill our supermarket shelves and we can reheat a meal in a matter of seconds ... just wait for the ping.

However, I also feel that we are moving back towards sensible eating (cake is always sensible and I won't hear otherwise). People have realized that eating foods in season gives the best flavor and is also much cheaper. There is a movement to recognize that animals need/should/must be kept in favorable and humane conditions and rightly so. I also think there is a leaning towards bringing herbal remedies back as well. Mother Nature provides incredibly strong medicine – always seek professional advice.

Perhaps we are following a cycle and coming back around to a more natural way of eating and living? Although I wouldn't want to go back to the days of not having inside toilets and hot showers I do think there is a huge merit to living in tune with the seasons especially when it concerns the food that we eat.

The wild woman/man would probably have had a field, woods and plenty of land available to plunder. As a modern kitchen witch, I do have a garden, it isn't large as I live on the edge of a big city in a terraced house but it has enough space to squeeze in some flowers, shrubs and plenty of herbs. I harvest and dry the flower petals, some leaves, seeds and all the herbs that I can. It doesn't matter how big your garden is, even a windowsill can hold a couple of pots of herbs. Growing and harvesting your own magical ingredients is incredibly rewarding including the time spent watching the bees and the butterflies enjoying it in situ too.

But, we don't all have the time or space for gardening so it is perfectly acceptable to purchase your herbs and spices from other sources. Farmers' markets are good but I would highly recommend finding out if you have an Asian supermarket nearby as they sell huge bags of herbs and spices at incredibly reasonable prices. All you have to do is come up with 100 magical ideas for the 2lb bag of sesame seeds you purchased because it was cheap ... ahem ...

Herbs bought from the supermarket are just as good to use as ones gathered yourself, all you need to do is give them a bit of a cleanse beforehand just to be sure. Anything purchased in a shop may have been handled by hundreds of people so it pays to give it a quick cleanse to remove any unwanted energy.

I have a personal issue with spells that have a list of ingredients as long as your arm and ones that include expensive items that you must order from across the other side of the world. In my mind, a kitchen witch will use whatever she has to hand and won't spend a lot of money on ingredients either. The original wise woman/man would have used items they found growing locally to them; they would not have had a supermarket or indeed the Internet to order fancy schmancy exotic spices from afar. And their magic worked perfectly ... look how many cows they successfully cursed?

Working with magical food is one of my favorite areas and when I say magical food I mean just food, you add the magic. Each and every item of food has magic within, even your microwave ready meal. As with all magical workings the important ingredient is your own will and intent. You can create a very special meal by adding in corresponding herbs and spices and using ingredients that relate to your intent. But you can also add in that intent by stirring; clockwise for positive energy or anti-clockwise to banish. Say a chant over the pot as you mix it, draw a symbol in your pastry or bread before you bake it. Or just charge your "instant meal for one" with your intent before you pop it in the microwave. You create the magic.

I also encourage you to make friends with your appliances, no I haven't gone mad (that is obviously up for debate). Our ancestors would have worked with only one or two pots that they used all the time for cooking. The modern kitchen witch works with any number of electric (or gas) gadgets and cupboards full of pots, pans and bowls. If you put positive energy into your kitchen and, furthermore, into the items that you use, it will transfer to your food and thus into your body. If you are bashing and stomping around the kitchen, slamming the fridge door and swearing at the oven door because it won't close properly then you are creating a very negative atmosphere that will probably result in a burnt or unappealing dinner. Be nice to your appliances, you don't have to give them pet names but treat them with respect and keep them clean and they will work nicely for you.

There is also the small matter of housework, ugh I know, it is one of those never ending relentless and often thankless tasks. But seriously if you make like Snow White on a regular basis (wouldn't it be nice if the woodland creatures actually did lend a hand?) it will benefit you. Creating a space that is free from dust and grime is not only good health and hygiene, especially in the kitchen, but it also allows the positive energy to flow.

I suspect the days of scrubbing kitchen floors and front door steps are long gone (thankfully). Along with sweeping all the floors with a besom to get rid of the straw. You can still sweep the house through even if you just do it symbolically, sweeping out negative energy with a besom works very well. The kitchen can also be given a magical cleanse. Pop a herbal tea bag or a few drops of essential oil in some hot water and wash your kitchen surfaces down with it. This can also be used on floor tiles or lino. Herbs have long been used strewn on the floors to get rid of bad smells and protect against illnesses such as the plague. Thankfully we don't need to protect against the plague now, but you can never be too sure. For carpet, you can create a herbal blend using dried herbs and spices ground up, sprinkle lightly over the floor and then vacuum up.

The hard work has been taken out of creating meals, we no longer have to get up at the crack of dawn to light the fire to heat the water and create the cooking area. Modern appliances are provided so you only have to flick a switch to mix your cake batter or knead your bread. One of my favorite appliances is my food mixer especially with the dough hook. You can still do it all by hand if you prefer but I don't see a problem in getting technology to do some of the work for you. You just say your magical chant over the food mixer as it turns.

Lotions and potions can be created within a modern fitted kitchen just as well, in fact, if not better. The Internet provides us with easy access to jars, bottles and ingredients with which to create them. No longer do we need to boil up animal fat to make soap or candles ... ewww.

We still use the natural items that our ancestors would have done. We bottle, can and preserve fruits from the hedgerows and vegetables from the garden. Soaps can be easily created from the "melt and pour" kits that are readily available, just add your own scent. Tinctures are still made mostly in the traditional manner. I love to mess about in my kitchen with herbs and spices to create my own loose incense blends, it is great fun.

But you don't need to be creative, I expect most of us know either personally or online someone who makes their own soaps, lotions and potions. It is lovely to be able to purchase items that have been handcrafted. And if it means I don't have to ruin several saucepans and burn myself with hot scalding wax (I speak from experience) then I am all for buying my candles online.

Does it matter if your candle was purchased from the pound/dollar store? Or does it need to be hand created by nymphs at midnight on the eve of the summer solstice to be more magical? In my personal experience, you source what you can afford and what you can lay your hands on easily. I repeat ... the magic is within you. Yes, it is lovely to be able to purchase handcrafted items but these aren't always affordable (and I totally understand and agree that the price is reflective of the time, energy, effort and quality ingredients used). A lot of people must work to an extremely tight budget. Use items that you can easily afford, then add in your own personal touches. Candles for instance can be dressed in oil and even that doesn't have to be essential oil, olive oil works very well indeed. Roll the candle in dried crushed herbs, stick on a few flower petals or tie a colored ribbon around it. All these ideas are cheap and easy to work with to bring in your own individual magic.

For me, being a kitchen witch means using items you have to hand, looking for magical ingredients in your kitchen cupboards and working the magic within the food you put on the table. It is about creating magic from things you already have and that don't cost the earth. There is a huge amount of magic to be found in a pebble from the beach. Soil from your garden has magic, even leaves from the tree in a city center park have a special spark of energy.

You don't have to live in a tumble-down cottage in the middle of the forest to be a witch. The modern-day witch can be found in city centers, suburbs, high rise flats, in the middle of housing estates, in fact anywhere at all! It doesn't matter where you live, the witch is within you.

Magic can be found all around even within the structure of a 1970s concrete office building. The land beneath us holds the magic of our ancestors, it carries the memories of each and every building that has stood there before it. Don't dismiss modern buildings or areas just because they seem "new." Whilst ancient sites hold ancient energy the newer buildings still stand on earth that is just as old. The city that I live in has a mixture of old and new buildings and a lot of concrete areas but it also has a sprinkling of parks and small green areas. But if you look back at the history, because it is a sea port it has had an infestation of human beings since the time of the cave man. Think about all the history, that is a lot of different cycles of not only humans and cultures but also buildings. Whilst the house I live in was built in 1920 it stands on a direct route that the Romans would have taken from the sea on their way to London. That is a vast number of ancestors traipsing up and down through my house ...

We may live in a world run by technology and whilst I am not convinced all of it is for the better, I do think that it is worthwhile embracing a lot of the modern ideas. We can make technology work for us. I am a kitchen/hedge witch who follows the old folk magic ways but I am one that embraces modern living. I love to pick plants and flowers from my garden to use for magic but I also love that I can bake those same magical ingredients into a cake inside my modern oven.

Sometimes it is good for my mental health and well-being to switch off the mobile phone and unplug the laptop. But without that modern technology this kitchen witch would not have been able to connect with all the other witches, druids and pagans across the globe. With the touch of a button I can be chatting with someone on the other side of the globe, I can see the images of their homes, families, gardens and magical endeavors. Who wouldn't want that kind of connection?

Old Craft for a
New Generation

Mélusine Draco

I recently read a response on an application form for Coven of the Scales to the question "What do you understand by the term traditional British Old Craft?"The response was that "'Witchcraft is whatever you want it to be?" It might if we are talking about eclectic paganism ... but within Old Craft if there is no natural ability for communicating with the spirit world, divination, recognizing and reading the omens, healing, cursing and moving between the worlds, then there is no witch. Added to this, Old Craft is extremely selective when it comes to prospective members and will reject any who prove themselves unsuitable for the Path.

Magic – whether of the folk or ritual variety – does not conform to the whims and vagaries of contemporary fashion and, like science, it has its own laws and lore that *must* be adhered to if a successful outcome is required. As ritual magician David Conway warns in his *The Complete Magic Primer,* to go through the ritual motions with no clear idea of what they are all about is mere superstition, not magic.

> In any case, the magician should expect more from his magic than mere signs and wonders. If these are all he is after, he would be better advised to take up conjuring, which is far less trouble. The real rewards of magical study are not temporal benefits but a spiritual maturity which affords a more profound understanding of the universe in which we live.

The form of traditional witchcraft practiced by the Coven of Scales teaches that the basic tenet of belief, although not a religion, does have a highly defined spiritual element to its practice. Also that traditional British Old Craft, like the mysteries of pre-dynastic Egypt and pre-Roman Italy, the ancestral beliefs of Japanese Shinto, the Aboriginals of Australia, and Native Americans is fundamentally animistic – the belief that every object, animate and inanimate, has its own life-force, or energy. Here there is no separation between the spiritual or physical world, where "spirit" exists in all flora and fauna (including humans); geological features such as rocks, mountains, rivers and springs; and in natural phenomena such as storms, wind and the movement of heavenly bodies. It is the understanding that a small quartz pebble can link us with the cosmic Divine.

Those members of CoS who have successfully passed through the first portal are usually mature individuals who have seriously studied other paths and traditions but were not comfortable with the contemporary dogma and questionable sources. Because let's make no bones about it, today's pagan interpretation of witchcraft often belongs to a revivalist tradition and should not claim to be anything else. Nevertheless, the seasonal rituals and celebrations need to be as close as they can to the beliefs of our Ancestors without falling into the trap of lumping all the deities together in one ageless pantheon ... and expecting the magic to work!

In order to follow the Old Ways, it is easier to understand if we reflect on the cornerstone of a witch's faith and ask ourselves those three-times-three basic questions:

What does a witch hold to be the three basic beliefs?
1. That there is one originating "force"
2. That this force is completely natural
3. That this natural force can be used by mankind

What does a witch ask for?
1. Sufficient nourishment (food and/or knowledge)

2. Shelter from the elements (also with a hidden meaning)
3. Love (again with hidden meaning)

What does a witch seek?
1. Knowledge, plus wisdom, plus understanding
2. Belief in tolerance and balance
3. The rule of natural law

These simple tenets of faith need to be enshrined in our memory because they allow us to perceive the simplicity at the heart of creation. That indefinable "something" which is impossible to grasp without the help of divinity, for it is beyond language, and yet it is so simple that we know that it is a part of us just as we are part of that which is enacted, that which is shown, and that which is spoken.

Much of this may be seen as playing with semantics, but in truth, the god-forms themselves have changed greatly down through the millennia. It is only by studying myths, legends and folklore, and pulling all the strands together that we can appreciate just how much these have altered. To a pre-dynastic Egyptian, for example, the goddess Isis was a modest deity identified with Osiris; later her cult spread into Greek and Roman society, becoming so popular in later days that she absorbed the qualities of many of the other deities – male *and* female. Early Christianity found it easier to incorporate the Mother and Child image into its own canon rather than suppress it; while in modern times she has become the greatly diluted Mother Goddess of international organizations – so far removed from the god-power of the ancient Nile valley that she would be seen as an alien entity by those early worshippers.

The spirits of the landscape that are the true focus of the ancestral beliefs of traditional British Old Craft have remained constant; they have not altered their form and have only grown more powerful with age. These well-springs of magical energy have not been contaminated because few have known of their existence – apart from the native shamanic practitioners [witches] who have kept the secret down through the ages. In more secluded spots, the spirit-energy of the ancient Britons survives in remote ancient monuments, isolated lakes, the rural landscape, and in the depths of the surviving wildwood with which our hunter-gatherer Ancestors would have been familiar. When the native shamanic practices went into the shadows, these powerful energy spots were deemed unholy and feared by the locals – and as such passed into folklore as those things that are "never fully remembered and yet never fully forgotten."

Those people who come to us are looking for the Path back to the Old Ways and learning how to connect with this timeless energy that "speaks" to them on a variety of different levels. And they come from all walks of life – there is an author, a senior fire officer, a lawyer, librarian, funeral director, a professional opera singer, a dance instructor, artist, animal-rights lawyer, sales executive, director of security, a psychology student – just sensible, erudite individuals who didn't want the easy option!

In the light of all this, it might be felt that traditional British Old Craft has no place in modern paganism since it *is* both elitist and hierarchical but our answer to that accusation has always been: "How can you teach yourself what you don't know exists?". And there's another very good reason why we do this, as Kenneth Grant explained so well in *Hecate's Fountain*:

It may be asked, why then do we not abandon the ancient symbols in favour of the formulae of nuclear physics and quantum mechanics? The answer is that the occultist understands that contact with these energies may be established more completely through symbols so ancient that they have had time to bury themselves in the vast storehouse of the racial subconsciousness. To such symbols the Forces respond swiftly and with incalculable fullness, whereas the pseudo-symbols manufactured in the laboratory possess no link with elements in the psyche to which they can appeal. The twisting and turning tunnels explored laboriously by science lead, only too often, away from the goal. The intellectual formulæ and symbols of mathematics have been evolved too recently to serve as direct conduits. For the Old Ones, such lines of communication are dead. The magician, therefore, uses the more direct paths which long ages have been mapped out in the shadowlands of the subconsciousness.

It is pointless stripping away all the ancient magical formulae to shoe-horn ancient wisdom into a pre-prescribed contemporary system in order to make it easier to understand, when the interior workings that drive the whole have been declared redundant. The ancient symbols, sigils, formulae, analogies and metaphors remain an integral part of the spiritual journey; just as magic is an amalgam of science and art and the stepping stone to the Mysteries. As Grant explains, these symbols are so ancient that they are firmly entrenched in the collective subconsciousness and it would be a mistake to discard them purely because they are not understood – or worse still – misunderstood.

During the recent BBC *History of Magic* program that unveiled rare books, manuscripts and magical objects from the British Library's collection and forthcoming exhibition, were revealed some of the traditions of folklore and magic which are at the heart of the Harry Potter stories. J K Rowling said of the exhibition:

The British Library has done an incredible job. Encountering objects for real that have in some shape or form figured in my books has been quite wonderful and to have several of my own items in the exhibition is a reminder of twenty amazing years since Harry was first published.

And she was honest enough to admit that although she had

thoroughly researched her subject, some of the magical stuff was made up!

The worlds of J K Rowling and J R R Tolkein are fabulous stories, full of magic and glamor (in the magical sense) but they are wonderful works of fiction and fantasy – not reality. Nevertheless I suspect that many of those original "kiddy converts" from twenty years ago have now grown up and swelled the pagan community but *where* do they go to discover authentic Old Craft. Our own "converts" discovered for themselves that there was a dearth of knowledgeable material available and it took them many years of searching before they discovered there were other approaches to traditional witchcraft than popular Wicca. Just as not every member of a Christian congregation came be a priest, so not every pagan can be a witch since according to tradition this is some innate ability that manifests in the ways of the Craft.

And although we draw upon the natural energy from the landscape, we are even closer to those sentient beings we refer to as the Ancestors who represent our culture, traditions, heritage, lineage and antecedents; they trace the long march of history that our predecessors have taken under the aegis of traditional British Old Craft. When those of a particular Tradition pass beyond the veil, their spiritual essence merges with the divine spirit of the Whole, which in turn gives traditional witchcraft the continuing power to endure – even past its own time and place in history. It therefore remains the duty of an Old Craft witch to ensure that the soul of any newly deceased can successfully join the Ancestors and keep adding to the strength of belief, which, in many instances may already have endured for hundreds of years. If when living, we cannot acknowledge and respect the Ancestors of traditional British Old Craft to which we *claim* to belong, then we will contribute nothing to the Whole when we die.

Reverence for Craft Ancestors is part of the ethic of respect for those who have preceded us in life, and their continued presence on the periphery of our consciousness means that they are always with us. And because traditional witchcraft is essentially a practical thing, the Ancestors are called upon to help find solutions to magical problems through divination, path-working and spell-casting. That is why we observe the "feast of the Ancestors" not at Samhain/Hallowe'en on 31ᵗ October but on 11 November when the time synchronizes with the Old Calendar because (to repeat the words of Kenneth Grant) we use the "more direct paths which long ages have been mapped out in the shadowlands of the subconsciousness."

This is not, however, the only time when the veil between the worlds is at its thinnest. There are several others in the witches' year and, like Old Samhain, Old Beltaine is also seen as a time, when the boundary between this world and the Otherworld could more easily be crossed and the "spirits" could more easily come into this world. In Old Craft we work with the old calendar dates that link us more closely with the Ancestors, because the further we move away from those Old Craft traditions we also cast aside the magical ties and techniques that have fueled Craft down through the ages.

And last, but certainly not least, we should never lose sight of the Path of the Hearth Fire and all its attendant superstitions, which often gets abandoned in the search for more loftier cosmic wisdom. The Hearth Fire is Love in *all* its various aspects; the source of womanly power and manly energy in its most sacred but most simplistic forms, and without it no other fire can come into existence. The Greeks (Hestia) and Romans (Vesta) had their goddesses of the Hearth and every home had its family altar on which offerings were made to the *lares familiaries*, the spirits who were particularly venerated at the domestic hearth on appropriate calendar days and on occasions of family importance. This is a warning that all would-be witches, *both male and female,* ignore at their peril. The friendly Hearth Fire is the symbol of domesticity and peace – and is the most precious of all.

So yes, in the twenty-first century you can view witchcraft as being whatever you want it to be but please don't pretend to be following the Old Ways – because those "old ways" still matter.

Twenty-First-Century Witches and the Arts

Dorothy Abrams

What is the witch's path in the twenty-first century? How is it unique? We know Witchcraft shapes and creates the reality of its age. We call this magic. We may also call it an art. Our creative inspiration makes rituals, spells, and community among the wise ones. We influence the health and wealth of the places we live. In this century we have a larger responsibility. A newly forged vision of witchcraft that is powerful, spiritual and beautiful must emerge from our past practices. The world needs us if it is to survive climate change, tyranny, greed and countless other crises. Because our earth is a dangerous place, we may work quietly or in secret but work we do.

Our work is a vision of an interaction between the Gods and Goddesses, the body and the soul. This two-way street blends spiritual breakthrough with the passion of beauty and dissonance found in the arts. Power thrums at a common beat to blend art and ritual. We are required to redefine both art and ritual in contemporary pagan experience. Witches hold on to the past ritual practices of sabbat and esabat and add a deeper understanding of what happens between the worlds. We demand more of ourselves and our Gods to shape spells and magic. We express that shaping with the arts. When our art is public, we use it to mold hope and love into powerful actions for the good of all. When our art is private, we seek to cast spells, create power vortices or reactivate the energy grids that crisscross the earth. We are serious in making a new reality.

Witches know creative inspiration has a spiritual source. Art comes from the internal soul when it works best. Some performers know what they do and others maybe not, but magic happens anyway. For example, I saw Rebecca Vaughan in her one woman show *I, Elizabeth*. I was thunderstruck as she channeled the great queen. The production is one act in 70 minutes, keeping Vaughan on stage throughout. Yet she aged without benefit of lighting or make up. She became Elizabeth. It was magic or time travel or both.

On another occasion I saw the Zamora family from New Mexico present a lyrical version of their Aztec fire rituals in full regalia that left me cowering in my seat. I must have unfinished business with their Gods. The spectacle was art and beauty and power. In the midst of the grandeur a small voice in my psyche was screaming "Oh no! They're back." I was transported by their dance and drums to another time when I was their subject. They played with fire and were not burned. At the end the lead dancer put out a flaming chalice with his bare foot without injury. I have no doubt that the ecstasy of spirit manifests itself in ritual magic and on stage. When the magic works it thrusts us into a union with the Gods and Goddesses in an ecstatic response.

As a result of the common ground beneath art and ritual I have helped fashion a community of witches and sundry pagans who express their beliefs through the visual arts (oils, watercolors, charcoal and pencil, or collage), writing (poetry, fiction, essays), dance (free form, belly dance and fire dances), three dimensional arts (sculpting, woodcrafts, charms, poppets and crafting), and music (performance, songwriting, transcription and arrangement). We named our group the Web PATH Center, PATH now standing for Pagan Arts, Teaching and Healing. Yes we conduct public rituals on the sabbats and moons, but we do more. We open up our creativity and make artists out of people who swore they were not creative. We use that creativity in group rituals and spells. Some of us continue exploration of the arts personally in performance, painting, crafting, stage or storytelling.

How do we do that? Education in Web PATH witchcraft

begins with a class *To Know the Magic*. People learn the basics of witchcraft: How to cast a circle, ground, call the quarters, evoke the deities and release the powers when the magic is completed. Students are asked to write their own ritual callings in free verse, poetry or as one student said "pretty words." Our point is that everyone is creative when infused with the spirit. Even in that introductory class people experience the pleasure of having words flow as magic happen on the page. We have poems and songs in our group repertoire now that were the results of this assignment and can be used by anyone in the group.

In our second level class *To Will the Magic* students are asked to channel a spiritual message through automatic writing. Some of those are ritual oriented. Others are God or Goddess stories, meditations, or wisdom literature. Once in a while with a particularly adept group we channel together. One person begins with a sentence or two and others add on until a full message is received. It has been a revelation in witches' truth.

Not to ignore the visual arts, students create a beautiful altar based on their astrological signs in partnerships with others of the same element. Fire signs find ways to represent earth, air and water from a fire perspective, and the same for the other elements. When the altars are done, students call the elementals in dance without words. Their movements change with the rhythms of fire, water, earth and air. Later in the second class we study magic. We make healing poppets. Most of these are cloth dolls. Some are wood or wax carvings. Then we charge them ritually and expect the healing to occur. Mostly it does.

In our third level class *To Dare the Magic* students learn storytelling. They confront their fears of public speaking and learn again that grounding is no abstract concept. It is the power that walks people through fear into achievement. The class ends in a dinner theater experience during which each student tells a God or Goddess story of their own choosing and creation complete with props, costuming and given without notes.

The public are invited. Not only are students developing keen presentation skills, they ally themselves with various deities in enduring ways. The stories often change their lives.

During the same class we look at Death. Students dance free form through a gate into the land of the dead and back. The experience takes on a strong significance with some students reluctant to move beyond the gate. They face their fears or their friends come and get them.

Part of daring the magic is appreciating our bodies, using them to form truth, individually or with partners. We may do mirror dancing to loosen up tight limbs and create comfort in eye contact. We make human sculptures based on provocative statements. The living statues' segment is part of a unit on the sacred clown. The group leader gives a team an assignment like: The child is father of the man (all credit to the Beach Boys and Wordsworth). The team is charged to think about what might be funny, backward or inside out to the words in a way that might challenge people's expectation. Then one person takes a pose center stage. A second one builds on that, and a third on that. They freeze in place and the class seeks to understand. We might end up with two men holding hands through a picture frame made of two other students. Or we might have a man in a birthing position and another in a fetal position beneath him held by others who are midwives. The limits are only in our brains.

In our fourth level class *To Keep Silent*, students create labyrinths in line drawings of their animal allies and familiars. A labyrinth follows the path inward to the center and back out without dead ends or tricks (that's a maze). Students create their own line drawings and meditative path. We then use them in meditation as a finger labyrinth. As part of the pagan exploration of prayer and contemplation they write their own pentacle meditation by lying in the form of a pentacle and channeling meaning and content from each of the points of the star as it would be drawn over them (invoking pentacle form). We write sacred dramas for a moon ritual or sabbat and then select the one to present to the Web.

Finally, in the fourth class students draw a circle mandala as simple or as complex as they wish. The initiation and celebration at the end includes a gallery showing of their visual arts. This particular class lasts a year and a day so there is time for the theme to present itself and ripen in their souls. One student made a sand mandala medicine wheel honoring her own Native American ancestors and the Tibetan tradition. She created it at the presentation, teaching her way through it. Then she ritually swept it away as a thing of impermanence.

The Web PATH Center opens the creative impulse in its members so that great things can happen. These new spiritual skills keep developing outside of the Web. Soft Moon Rising was given an opportunity to work with a county-wide mural project even though she had no experience in oils and drawing. Because she paints walls, someone asked her to come and prepare the large canvasses for the public murals. When she arrived someone else had done that so she was asked if she could paint a deer. Turns out she could. Who knew? Now she teaches spirit drawing as a divination tool, as well as painting commissioned work and continuing with the mural project and public art. I particularly like her benches at the Garden of Hope in Lyons, NY. She credits the Reiki attunements that accompanied the classes in witchcraft with opening her creative vision and giving her confidence.

Soft Moon Rising is also a self-taught bass guitarist. She inherited her country band when the leader unexpectedly passed. Sometimes she and I work music together. One Solstice, the two of us created an entire ritual in song, most of them original. She wrote the lyrics and melody. I arranged the harmonies and taught the parts to a Web PATH choir aptly named The Herded Cats. The ritual had all the usual elements of witches' circles but all the workings were set to music. At the time we had enough strong voices to carry the ritual forward in three-and four-part harmony. I told her I wanted to sing and she could direct the choir. She had never done that before. I laughed. Spirit worked it out. She was great.

Zatira has a full set of crystal singing bowls. She conducts ritual by playing them. Their vibrations transport even the most blocked consciousness out of its body into the spirit realm. Although she will use the usual method of running the wand around the rim to set a bowl singing its one note, she also uses a soft mallet to strike them like bells, combining the notes in pleasing harmony and dissonance, resolving them into chords. At one point I felt the pull of my spirit lover and was halfway out of my body into the next realm before some spirit overruled us. The bowls played this way have deep healing powers. The third eye bowls enhance psychic insight and heal vision problems.

Finally some of our best crafters teach us knot magic or other sleight of hand workings when it is their turn to lead the full moon rites. I am cack-handed when it comes to crafting, so I give it my all but it usually leaves a good deal to the imagination. I call them my abstract art projects. Only Spirit and I know what it is and what it means. That may be as it should be. I do have a special woven charm necklace made under the full moon thanks to Cindy who brought the yarns and moon charms so we could create something beautiful together.

One of my favorite rituals involved such a working and a cauldron of water for scrying. We made the charms and were charging them on the altar one by one. The room was dimly lit so one of us tripped over the cauldron and spilled the water across the carpet. We mopped it up with towels and left them in place. The trail formed a river of consciousness over one side of the room which had to be crossed as best as one could. Somehow that simple accident made a deep meditative experience deeper for people who were resisting some personal truth. Their privacy was protected but the physical act of stepping over the water made them feel like it was the River Styx. Their struggle became clear and supported by the group even though we were not privy to the details.

That's the fascinating part about spirit art. You never know what you are going to get or how the plot twist will happen. We were celebrating the full moon when the Goddess told me in a meditation to write a book on sacred sex. I didn't want to do that. I told the circle about my message and my reluctance. Galadriel said quite innocently "What if we all wrote it?" Not long after, Trevor Greenfield our editor here at Moon Books asked if anyone was interested in writing a book on sacred sex and there we were. *Sacred Sex and Magick* was published by my circle in 2015. None of them had written a book before but we did together. If nearly 20 people can collaborate on a book and have no disputes, finishing the works as good as friends as they were in the beginning, then that is witchcraft!

This season the web witches who also practice shamanism are including graphic arts with their shamanic journeys. We begin with the spirit animal labyrinths and trust our guides to direct us to new ventures in shamanic art. Some of that will be set to change the world. Our Intensive last September focused on the consciousness of Gaia. We dedicate our workings to her evolution and ours as a human race along with her. Some of that may appear in the Web Coloring Book soon to be available through our website.

As pagans, artists, teachers and healers, the Webfolk are serious and comical about ourselves and our workings. We see the path we forge in the twenty-first century as one in which people make magic from the simplest things around us to the most profound. We do it slyly with paintings or performances. We raise people's energy with sound. We create hope for a finer future when the way forward seems warlike. We ask the spirits to make art through us, to weave us together into a stronger family. We channel messages in words or drawings. We make poppets to forge a connection between what is and what is imagined. We expect our visions to be manifest. And so it shall be.

Casting Your Own Circle

Arietta Bryant

A modern practitioner of Witchcraft and Magick has many choices available to them. You can work Solitary, as a Hedge or Kitchen Witch, you can practice within a Coven setting, you can join an online group, or you could attend Open Circles.

When I first began to take an academic interest in Magick and, specifically for me, the spirituality of Wicca, there was a limit to what information could be found locally. This was a time before the easy networking of social media, before online forums, and before personal email accounts. However, this lack of ready communication with others of a like mind did lead me to be a voracious reader of everything I could get my hands on with regards to Magick, Witchcraft, and Wicca. Through reading so much from so many different authors I was able to get a really well-rounded picture of all that was available for me.

In the early days of my reading, I found good quality Magick books hard to come by in my local shops and this encouraged me to read around the subjects I was interested in. I read books on cookery and gardening to further my knowledge of potions. I read up on Astrology and looked into disciplines like Phrenology and Graphology, which were popular as parlor-games and therefore socially acceptable in a non-Pagan setting. I studied Psychology and Sociology at night school. I also gathered quite a collection of books containing Celtic myths and faerie tales, and I always kept my eyes peeled in our local charity shops for any works of fiction which might have a magical theme. It is surprising how much truth you find in some fictions!

As a Solitary Witch, I was quite happy doing my own thing, which was cobbled together, from the bits I had felt a connection with, in the books I had studied. With no "peers" to judge me,

I celebrated the Sabbats, worked spells and felt my personal connection to the Divine strengthening. At that time, I didn't consider myself a follower of any particular Tradition because I had no lineage. I do recall seeing the term "Eclectic Witch" in a few books but I didn't feel the need to label myself as such at that stage.

By the time that I was 21, the Internet had become more accessible. I found I could reach out to others online and I began formal training as a Wiccan Priestess with the Crystal Waterfall Coven. Following the completion of my training, I set up a small "working group" called The Never-Ending Circle. Our practices mostly followed the training I had undertaken with some additional influence from prominent Magickal authors such as Titania Hardie, Raymond Buckland, Scott Cunningham, and Amber K, to name just a few.

It was during this same time-period that I also started attending our local Pagan Pub Moot and really began to feel that I had become a part of the wider magickal community. Through this newfound community, I had the opportunity to speak to people from a great variety of paths and traditions. Druids, Witches, Spiritualists, and Shamans all had their own knowledge to share with me and it all seemed relevant and useful.

One of the contacts I made through the moots was an American Witch with whom I spent a brief time studying the American Wiccan Tradition known as "Blue Star." The Blue Star tradition, which was formed in the 1970s by Frank Dufner, has many elements which I admire. There is an emphasis on family and there is a regular inclusion of original music and song in their rituals. I spent a long time trying to make Blue Star Wicca fit me but ultimately it was not to be, although I was sad to leave the music behind.

I began to understand that spirituality was a really personal affair. It was not one-size-fits-all, and it seemed that nothing I had discovered so far really fit the bill for me. I continued my solitary eclectic practices, I attended Pagan Moots, and most importantly, I continued to read.

In 2002, with the support of a few friends, I succeeded in setting up a public Open Circle to celebrate the Sabbats and offer workshops where we could all share our knowledge, and for a time this was sufficient to fulfill my personal spiritual needs. Even if it was a little inconsistent.

For anyone interested in setting up an Open Circle I would say "Do it!" When I began this venture, the circles were only advertised by word of mouth, and hand printed leaflets given to local new-age shops and health stores. So, with all the networking available through social media today, it should be easier than ever to get folks to come along to your events.

When the idea of setting up an open circle first took seed, I began by looking for an area of land which I thought could work for us. I then contacted our local council, in writing, to ask for permission to use the space. They invited me for a face to face meeting (which included them asking me if we would be sacrificing anything! – I am still not sure if they were serious or not) and telling us that we would need public liability insurance to the tune of three million pounds. So, once our insurance was in place we were very lucky to be offered an even better venue than the one I had originally suggested to them. We gave the council members an open invite to pop along to a ritual at any time. But they never did.

It was early in 2005 when I; and my Sister Witch, Romany Rivers, decided to pool our knowledge, and our resources, and found our own tradition. We had both been approached by several people looking for magickal and spiritual training and decided that together we would be able to create a training framework. This grew into a tradition that reflects the past but is grounded in the modern world.

We began by looking at our own everyday practices. We both kept diaries, detailing those little magickal acts which had crept into the fabric of our everyday. We were surprised just how much magick we performed. There were morning devotions; whether they are taken while kneeling at an altar, or whilst grabbing a quick morning shower. Conscious decisions to stir our tea in a clockwise direction, and on some occasions, boosting the spell by stirring in a pentagram too. Favorite foods which we attributed to different Pagan holidays, and for both of us, we found that poetry, song, and storytelling were important triggers in both ritual and spell casting.

Many a pot of tea was drunk whilst we sat and pored through our collection of books, notes, and personal books of shadows. I do recall it being a little overwhelming, trying to pull together the fragments of our own practices into a coherent tradition which both of us could say we believed in and which could still be relevant to another person's spiritual needs. To help us to understand the task a little better we looked at the etymology of the word "Tradition" and saw that in its simplest form it means to "give across" or to "pass on" information and ideas. This then gave us a strong starting point where we came up with a central core of principles which could be "passed on" to new students.

If you decide you would like to follow our example and form a new tradition then I would recommend you doing similar activities like keeping a diary of your regular magickal (and mundane) activities and coming up with a core set of principles, values, or beliefs. Of course, the values which you choose for your tradition might not be exactly the same as those of Moon River Wicca, just the same way that the core principles of Blue Star Wicca are not exactly the same as Gardnerian or Alexandrian Wicca. Most magickal paths will share some common ground but it is their points of uniqueness which set them apart.

The Moon River Wicca Principles were broken down into a series of headings for ease of teaching them to others and I have included a short description of each here, but during our classes, we expand upon these points in much greater depth and have had some very lively debates with students about some of these concepts. You could use these headings as a jumping off point for creating principles of your own:

Acceptance of all – We welcome all, and will not tolerate prejudice of any kind towards ourselves of others.

Tolerance of Diversity – We realize that not everyone will experience the Divine the way that we do, we do not believe that there is "one true way" rather that there are many paths to our own truths.

The Concept of Evil – We believe that a conscious act of harm is the only true evil. Whilst we recognize the polarity in all things we do not believe there to be an ultimate evil which is in direct opposition to an ultimate good.

Morals & Ethics – We believe a person can live honestly without the "threat" of spiritually enforced punishment, or reward. However, we strive to live with "Harm to None" and believe that, energetically, what we put out into the world shall be returned to us.

Self-Responsibility – This one follows on nicely from Morals & Ethics. We believe that we are each responsible for our own actions and that all "Karmic Debts" should be balanced in this lifetime. We feel that the key to Self-Responsibility is to "Know Thyself" and to be aware of our shadow as well as our light.

Living by Example – Whilst we do not proselytize we are a teaching tradition and our philosophy within a student/ teacher setting should always be one whereby we aim to learn something from our students in an exchange of knowledge.

We also believe that whilst Initiation should always be free, it is right and proper for a tutor of Moon River Wicca to charge for their time and any other expenses incurred whilst they are running a class or workshop. As agreed between the Teacher and the Student, this could be either financial or some other material or energetic exchange.

The Polarity of Divinity – We see the Divine source as both Male and Female. Both are revered equally and although some festivals may have a focus on either the Masculine or the Feminine aspects of the Divine, we do recognize that they both play a part in all festivals. The names used to address the aspects of the Divine are personal choices for each follower of the Moon River Path, but in a group setting often we will use the terms "Lord" and "Lady" for ease of understanding.

The Cyclical Nature of Energy – Energy is in everything, it does not die, it merely transmutes. Every part of everything is made of energy. It follows then that we are ourselves energetically connected to all that has gone before, and we contain within us sparks of the future itself. We all hold some part of the divine energy within us. We are all God and Goddess.

Magick, Crafting, Casting & Divination – Knowing that everything can be broken down into energy, means that we can also impact this energy with our own will. We call this Magick. Magick of any kind must be performed with a clear intent and within the bounds of our personal moral and ethical code. We encourage all our students to research and practice a range of different skills and techniques for both spell casting and divination.

Reincarnation – We believe that our "personal energetic

signature," or "life force" will continue on after our death to rest in the Summerland. In the Summerland, we are stripped of our ego and re-joined to the universal consciousness. Then after an indeterminable time, our life force will be reborn into a new body. We also believe that we will meet again with those we have known and loved before, and these people are called "Soul Mates."

Personal Spirituality – We cannot walk your path for you and as such it is up to followers of the Moon River Path to create their own personal spin on our ideas. The Moon River framework gives you core beliefs around which you can carve out your own path. We want all of the Moon River Wiccans to "know thyself." We do not insist on you recreating everything exactly the same way that we do it, our way might not work for you, your way may, in fact, be better.

Continuing the theme of Personal Spirituality, one thing which was really important to us when we set out our tradition was that each Moon River Wiccan should be free to work in a Coven or Solitary setting, and within any pantheon in which they felt comfortable, so long as they respected our core principles.

Followers of the Moon River Tradition should ritually acknowledge every full moon, and also celebrate the following festivals:

Samhain, a balanced festival, on 31 October
Yule (Midwinter), a God festival, on 21 December
Imbolc, a Goddess festival, on 2 February
Ostara (Spring Equinox), a Goddess festival, on 21 March
Beltane, a balanced festival, on 30 April and 1 May
Litha (Midsummer), a God festival, on 21 June
Lughnasadh (Lammas), a God festival, on 31 July
Mabon (Autumn Equinox), a Goddess festival, on 21 September

Once we had settled on our core principles we began offering Moon River training, following a degree system, to small groups with the option of them taking part in an Initiation Ritual upon completion.

Our degree system is broken down into levels. They are Seeker, Dedicant, First-Level Initiate, Second-Level Initiate, Third-Level Initiate, and Elder. Each level takes a minimum of a year and a day to complete. Offering tiered teaching, through a degree system, is a fairly traditional way to train in a coven setting but it also worked for us because it gave us a way to offer structured training which was understandable to everyone. For instance, if you wanted to learn about the basics of Wicca and Witchcraft, then you could take our Seeker level course and come away with all the basic knowledge you would get from any "Wicca 101" course, and more besides. You could then choose to attend Initiation, or you could continue to walk a different path.

This beautiful and diverse tradition has become a bridge between Eclectic Wicca and the more structured traditions. Moon River Wicca has become so much more than we ever believed possible, and to this day it continues to evolve. If you can't find what you are looking for in the books, websites, or teachings of others, then today's modern Witch can and should feel free to create their own path. Craft your own personal spirituality, cast your own circle.

Cows and Crows: A Celtic Perspective

Mabh Savage

We often focus on the modernity of current Witchcraft; how to make it work in a modern age by changing its shape and form to fit in with our ever changing, technology based lifestyles. Spells are worked over the Internet, with Facebook groups allowing those who have never seen each other to work together for the greater good. Twitter allows us to search the "Pagan" tag for likeminded folk; or flame those whose methods we don't agree with. Modern transportation means that the most sacred of stone circles is only hours away for most people, if they have the money and can get time off from the day job. My friend runs a very successful crystal business purely over the Internet, and another gives readings the same way; helping people they never, ever meet with their spiritual lives. Magic and witchcraft have transformed in ways our ancestors could only dream of, and you can either see this as moving away from our ancestral heritage, or as an evolution of it.

I generally prefer to concentrate on the latter statement; as I say over and over, we are not our ancestors. If our ancestors had enjoyed access to our science and technology, no doubt they would have used it to the maximum of its abilities too. There is no shame in utilizing social media, email, cars, public transportation, computers and so forth to further your magical practice. You use what you have, just as the ancient Greeks used magnetic lodestones to add drama to spell casting (*Papyri Graecae Magicae* (*PGM*)).

But what about when you want to get a closer feel for the magic your ancestors may have experienced? When you want to take a step away from our technological maelstrom, into the chaos of nature and the raw universe? This is when we reverse the meaning of modern witchcraft; where we stop trying to make our witchcraft fit in to the modern world, and instead strip back our modern lives to better fit the older, wilder meaning of witchcraft. This is my favorite part of my path; the part I tend to refer to as Celtic Witchcraft, where I return to the myths and legends of my Irish ancestors for inspiration for my magic, and lose myself in wild and unkempt woods, wastelands and waters, always keeping an ear and an eye out for the aos sídhe, partly out of fascination and partly out of self-preservation; they don't generally mean us well.

Translating Celtic deities into a modern setting has caused debate amongst pagan circles for years. The Morrígan is a prime example. Remember the "bullets for the Morrígan" controversy? Some worshippers of the Great Queen(s) decided that bullets were a modern version of swords and therefore suitable tribute for a goddess of war. Some found this distasteful, seeing guns as holding no value other than to take life, whereas a blade has many metaphorical layers of meaning; to cut away unwanted parts of one's life, for example, or to whittle something into shape. Others saw guns and bullets as symbols of protection, and still others saw them as symbols of freedom.

It cannot be denied that the Morrígan is closely linked to violence; horrible, bloody violence at times. But what's fascinating is the way different worshippers deal with this. Some try and minimize this part of her. Others glorify it. Others still, and this is more where I fit in, try and see the balance; she absolutely is a war goddess and absolutely represents violence, but this is not all she is, and if you don't respect her as a full "person," a well rounded, multi-faceted goddess, then you might be called out for being disrespectful, and no one wants to be called out by the Morrígan!

I've never personally offered weaponry to the Morrígan (no judgment if you have, let me make that clear; your magic is your own and no one can take that away from you) as I find another way to connect with her on a daily basis, even in my little, suburban corner of Yorkshire.

Crows

Simple as that, my friends; the black corvids she is so closely linked to, in so many tales, are rife across our planet, and live harmoniously with us dirty, filthy humans. They are our cleaners; our winged staff, eating the carrion, clearing up the rubbish and generally making the world a nicer smelling place, one scrap at a time.

The links between the mighty Morrígan and this most common of scavengers are littered (ahem) throughout Irish Celtic tales.

In the Wood of Badb, i.e. of the Morrigu, for that is her wood, viz. the land of Ross, and she is the Battle-Crow and is called the Wife of Neit, i.e. the Goddess of Battle, for Neit is the same as God of Battle.

This tiny excerpt from *The Wooing of Emer* gives us a wealth of information about the Morrígan, including her links to Badb, her perceived nature as a Goddess and her title (again, via Badb) of Battle-Crow.

In the tale of Odras, from *The Metrical Dindshenchas,* the Dagda's wife, a "shape-shifting goddess," referred to later in the tale as the Morrígan, is named as a "raven-caller," implying a strong connection with or power over the magnificent corvids.

Also in *TMD,* Macha, again, strongly connected with the Morrígan, is named as "raven of the raids" (Source: *The Metrical Dindshenchas,* tr. Edward Gwynn, CELT, UC, Cork, 2005).

These are just a drop of blood in a huge body of tales that links the Morrígan to the animal world, and in particular to crows, ravens and rooks. The amazing thing about seeing a crow today is that you are seeing, in many ways, the same bird your Celtic forebears might have been eyeing up over a thousand years ago.

On the way to battle, a single crow hulking in a hawthorn tree by the side of the track could have been seen as a very ill omen. Then again, depending on your relationship with the Goddess(es) of war, perhaps it was a very good omen indeed? Likewise, even today, we can choose to see these shadowy creatures as portents of darkness and doom, or symbols of darkness and reflection; introspection; transformation.

There's no denying the birds' connection to death, the underworld and the boundaries between dimensions. But just like the tarot card of death, we don't *have* to take everything quite so literally. In fact, in witchcraft, symbolism and metaphor are extremely important, and allow us to focus our intent in ways that may not otherwise be possible.

Just as the Morrígan is not *only* a war goddess, so the crows are not simply scavengers, lost in a world of blood and broken bodies. They symbolize searching; striving; family life; close bonds; change; mystery, and magic itself.

When I pray to the Morrígan, I imagine great black wings rising on my back. I feel the air beating down and though my feet never leave the ground I am soaring, high on my own ambition and the connection to the Goddess. I feel the strength of the midnight plumage as these wondrous wings drive me forward towards my goal. I know it is my own strength that the goddess is helping me find, but my connection to her is the catalyst. I reach out to her, and she reminds me to look inwards as well as outwards to find my solutions.

My own offerings are all items that are readily available from modern-day shops, although I try and keep them as "natural" as possible, keeping in mind that my modern witchcraft ties back to the much older magic, and may have to survive well into a future deprived of resources we take for granted today.

- Candles, preferably red, preferably beeswax.
- Mead, any is fine but my magical sister Kath's homebrew

is my favorite!

- Feathers; crow or rook are local to me but raven would be amazing too.
- Incense; I have always found dragon's blood potent.
- The colors red, black and white.

Honoring a goddess is a very personal affair. If you meet the Morrígan, you are likely to do so treading a very different path to mine. I am happy that I have come to know this sometimes elusive and always transformative Goddess through the birds that are so beloved to me and so sacred to her.

The Morrígan is just one example of a Celtic deity who is often sought out today still. There are, of course, so many more, such as the Dagda, associated with clubs and cauldrons, life, death and rebirth. Lugh of the long arm, who we honor every time we learn and then master a new skill. The techniques for either seeing these ancient beings in a modern setting, or conversely removing ourselves from the modern setting to liaise more firmly with our gods, can be carried over to any pantheon and any path. Meditation, visualization and pathworking are also very valid ways of making contact with spirits and gods, when the pressures of a modern world just seem to build barriers that prevent that level of connection.

We can't "unwilden" our Gods and Goddesses; we must re-wilden ourselves. We shouldn't try and ignore their connections to animals, the seasons and the natural world just to make our deities "fit" into our modern setting. We should, instead, honor these signs and symbols where we see them, and if we cannot remove ourselves physically from the urban landscape, we should study the tales and mythology of our chosen Gods and Goddesses and try and connect with those deities through dreams, meditation, retelling the tales, song, poetry, and other skills that bind heart, spirit and mind together.

Celtic mythology isn't just about Gods and Goddesses of

course, in fact, many of the protagonists appear to be "normal" people, or supernatural at a level which isn't deity, such as *sidhe* (fairy), or part god, such as Cú Chulainn.

My namesake is Medb, queen of Connacht, who is possibly (but not definitely) a goddess at some point in her mythology. She is a lady who I find much in common with, if that doesn't smack too much of arrogance! She finds it incredibly unfair that her husband should even think that he has more wealth than her. She doesn't want more; she just wants to be equal, a sentiment that many of us (men and women) including myself, echo to this day. Like me, she is wilfully stubborn, and if she believes she is in the right, won't let go. Also, in some tales, she was killed with a piece of cheese, which sounds exactly like the ridiculous type of thing that would happen to me.

Medb, very famously, appears in *Táin Bó Cúailnge*, often known simply as "The Táin." This is a great story as it highlights another type of common animal that was important to the Irish Celts, and still symbolizes wealth and power today: cattle. In *The Táin* there's a rather large scrap fought over a bull, the famous Donn Cúailnge (Dun Bull of Cooley). The bull represents the tipping point in whether husband or wife will be the wealthiest. His value is so high, he would place one party firmly above the other, were they to win him.

I see cattle every day where I live, as we are on the edge of a city that borders rural Yorkshire, and so are surrounded by farmland. Through reading tales such as *The Táin,* both cows and bulls have come to symbolize many themes which echo throughout history and will always be relevant in any era: having the courage to fight for what you believe should be yours; stubbornness; willfulness (both the bad behavior type of willfulness and the literal interpretation of acting upon your will) and also from the tale of Medb and Ailill, they speak to me of equality and fighting for that equality, although there is also the inherent cautionary tale of the dangers of one-upmanship.

Clearly, even today, cows and bulls still very much represent money and wealth. Bullocks are raised to adulthood for beef and leather. Cows are raised for milk, and so butter, cheese, yoghurt and all that goes along with that. Thus cattle are a literal representation of worth, in an extremely meat and dairy based society that shows little sign of wavering in the face of a growing wave of veganism. Again, that's not a value judgment, simply a fact of current Western society.

There are, of course, cows and bulls which are kept neither for milk nor meat, but simply because they are beautiful creatures. Some smaller farms near us keep rare breeds of cattle, partly for the curiosity factor, partly to stop those breeds dying out and partly because the owners have a passion for the beasts that surpasses the "what can they do for us" mentality that many humans hold regarding what they perceive as "livestock." Instead of the animal's worth being measured in the revenue they can generate, the animal *is* the worth; the wealth.

This is closer to echoing the Celtic ideal of kept animals. Although the animals did have monetary value (in the sense that they could be used for trade with a high value), they were also revered simply as the beautiful and often magical creatures they were. The Morrígan herself is known to have transformed into a cow; a white, red-eared heifer, the colors signifying the magical nature of the beast and her connection to the supernatural. She also visited the famous Donn in the form of a crow, another example of her connection to the corvids, and another indication that the cow and the bull are her sacred animals, as well as being magnificent and magical in their own right.

The cattle at the rare breeds' farms do bring literal wealth too, through encouraging visitation to the farm by other curious cattle fans. Yes, that includes me, and the kids. I still have an awesome photo of my little boy at three years old, delightedly feeding grass he had plucked to a jet-black Dexter cow. Interestingly, this particular breed can also be dun or red, much like many of the cattle from the Celtic tales. It's strange how the familiar symbolism keeps popping up, once you are aware of it.

Returning to the Celtic Queen I am named for; I have never actively searched for Medb in my magic or meditations, although it's possible I may have encountered her unknowingly, as she has been conflated with the Morrígan at times. Am I afraid to seek my namesake? A little, yes. I believe that we should always be open (with ourselves) about our fears, as if we can't recognize a thing, how can we confront it? I had no choice over my naming, but I am grateful for it and the strength it symbolizes. One day, I will honor it further and seek out the Celtic forebear of my (slightly anglicized) name, and won't that be something to write about ...

Contributors

Amie Ravenson is a long-time eclectic, intuitive, solitary witch and tarot reader who lives in Lawrenceville, GA with her husbear Josef, three cats, and more books than any one person should reasonably own. You can find her at www.AmieRavenson.com, where you'll find links to her podcast, YouTube channel, and Etsy shop.

Annette George lives in the rural Highlands of Scotland, an incomer from her home county of Wiltshire. A solitary, eclectic Pagan and Hedge Witch, she is contributor to *Paganism 101* and *Witchcraft Today 60 Years On*. She currently blogs for Moon Books and also on her Facebook page, Highland Hedge Witch. A lover of nature's wild places and all their elemental magical beauty, she writes about matters close to home and to her heart, and about her journey on her pagan path.

Arietta Bryant has been a practicing pagan for over twenty years. She is co-founder of Moon River Wicca, a progressive Wiccan tradition, offering classes and courses both locally and internationally. She is a contributor to *Naming the Goddess, Pagan Planet* and *Every Day Magic*. Arietta lives, in Hampshire, UK.

Dorothy Abrams is the co-founder of the Web PATH Center, a pagan church and teaching facility in Lyons, New York, USA. She is the author of *Identity and the Quartered Circle: Studies in Applied Wicca* and also contributed to *Paganism 101, Naming the Goddess, Witchcraft Today 60 Years On,* and *The Goddess in America*. She is the editor of *Sacred Sex and Magick* by the Web PATH Center.

Irisanya Moon is a Reclaiming Witch, initiate, priestess, international teacher, and drummer, as well as an often-vegan, shapeshifter, shadow stalker, invocateur, and Sagittarius devoted to Aphrodite, Iris, Hecate, and the Norns. She has been published in *Paganism 101, Naming the Goddess, Pagan Planet,* and *Goddess in America* and makes her living in California as a writer and magick maker. www.irisanya.com

Mabh Savage lives in Yorkshire, England. She is involved with several pagan groups and explores her heritage as a way to get closer to her ancestors and the world around her. She is the author of *A Modern Celt* and *Celtic Witchcraft.*

Mélusine Draco originally trained in the magical arts of traditional British Old Craft with Bob and Mériém Clay-Egerton. She has been a magical and spiritual instructor for over 20 years with Arcanum and the Temple of Khem. She is the author of a number of books including the popular *Traditional Witchcraft* series. She lives in Ireland near the Galtee Mountains.

Morgan Daimler is a blogger, poet, teacher of esoteric subjects, witch, and priestess of the Daoine Maithe. She lives in Connecticut, USA and is the author of a number of books including *The Morrigan, Fairycraft,* and *Odin.*

Philipp J. Kessler (RevKess) is the author of the "Dark of the Moon, New Beginnings" series from Saturn Returns Publishing, cohost of the Pagan-Musings Podcast on BlogTalkRadio, Murphy's Magic Mess, and Lavender Hill on KZUM.org. He has been included in anthologies from Immanion Press-Megalithica Books. He can be reached at authorrevkess@gmail.com.

Rachel Patterson is High Priestess of the Kitchen Witch Coven and an Elder of the Kitchen Witch School of Natural Witchcraft. A Green/Kitchen Witch with an added dash of hedgewitch and folk magic, she is also the author of a number of books including

Kitchen Witchcraft, Moon Magic and *Witchcraft ... into the wilds*. She lives in Portsmouth, UK.

Rebecca Beattie lives in London and is a PhD candidate at the University of Middlesex, where she is researching and writing a novel about Mary Webb. She has previously written two novels, *The Lychway*, and *Somewhere She Is There*, and a book of short stories, *The Softness of Water*. Rebecca is also the author of *Nature Mystics; The Literary Gateway to Modern Paganism*.

MOON

BOOKS

PAGANISM & SHAMANISM

What is Paganism? A religion, a spirituality, an alternative
belief system, nature worship? You can find support for all these
definitions (and many more) in dictionaries, encyclopaedias, and
text books of religion, but subscribe to any one and the truth will
evade you. Above all Paganism is a creative pursuit, an encounter
with reality, an exploration of meaning and an expression of the
soul. Druids, Heathens, Wiccans and others, all contribute their
insights and literary riches to the Pagan tradition. Moon Books
invites you to begin or to deepen your own encounter, right here,
right now.
If you have enjoyed this book, why not tell other readers by
posting a review on your preferred book site.

Recent bestsellers from Moon Books are:

Journey to the Dark Goddess
How to Return to Your Soul
Jane Meredith
Discover the powerful secrets of the Dark Goddess and
transform your depression, grief and pain into healing
and integration.
Paperback: 978-1-84694-677-6 ebook: 978-1-78099-223-5

Shamanic Reiki
Expanded Ways of Working with Universal Life Force Energy
Llyn Roberts, Robert Levy
Shamanism and Reiki are each powerful ways of healing; together,
their power multiplies. *Shamanic Reiki* introduces techniques to
help healers and Reiki practitioners tap ancient healing wisdom.
Paperback: 978-1-84694-037-8 ebook: 978-1-84694-650-9

Pagan Portals – The Awen Alone
Walking the Path of the Solitary Druid
Joanna van der Hoeven
An introductory guide for the solitary Druid, *The Awen Alone* will
accompany you as you explore, and seek out your own place
within the natural world.
Paperback: 978-1-78279-547-6 ebook: 978-1-78279-546-9

A Kitchen Witch's World of Magical Herbs & Plants
Rachel Patterson
A journey into the magical world of herbs and plants, filled with
magical uses, folklore, history and practical magic. By popular
writer, blogger and kitchen witch, Tansy Firedragon.
Paperback: 978-1-78279-621-3 ebook: 978-1-78279-620-6

Medicine for the Soul
The Complete Book of Shamanic Healing
Ross Heaven
All you will ever need to know about shamanic healing and how to
become your own shaman...
Paperback: 978-1-78099-419-2 ebook: 978-1-78099-420-8

Shaman Pathways – The Druid Shaman
Exploring the Celtic Otherworld
Danu Forest
A practical guide to Celtic shamanism with exercises and
techniques as well as traditional lore for exploring the Celtic
Otherworld.
Paperback: 978-1-78099-615-8 ebook: 978-1-78099-616-5

Traditional Witchcraft for the Woods and Forests
A Witch's Guide to the Woodland with Guided Meditations and
Pathworking
Mélusine Draco
A Witch's guide to walking alone in the woods, with guided
meditations and pathworking.
Paperback: 978-1-84694-803-9 ebook: 978-1-84694-804-6

Wild Earth, Wild Soul
A Manual for an Ecstatic Culture
Bill Pfeiffer
Imagine a nature-based culture so alive and so connected,
spreading like wildfire. This book is the first flame...
Paperback: 978-1-78099-187-0 ebook: 978-1-78099-188-7

Naming the Goddess
Trevor Greenfield
Naming the Goddess is written by over eighty adherents and
scholars of Goddess and Goddess Spirituality.
Paperback: 978-1-78279-476-9 ebook: 978-1-78279-475-2

Shapeshifting into Higher Consciousness
Heal and Transform Yourself and Our World with Ancient
Shamanic and Modern Methods
Llyn Roberts
Ancient and modern methods that you can use every day to
transform yourself and make a positive difference in the world.
Paperback: 978-1-84694-843-5 ebook: 978-1-84694-844-2

Readers of ebooks can buy or view any of these bestsellers by
clicking on the live link in the title. Most titles are published in
paperback and as an ebook. Paperbacks are available in traditional
bookshops. Both print and ebook formats are available online.

Find more titles and sign up to our readers' newsletter at
http://www.johnhuntpublishing.com/paganism
Follow us on Facebook at https://www.facebook.com/MoonBooks
and Twitter at https://twitter.com/MoonBooksJHP

·

Printed and bound by PG in the USA